STAMPABILITY

CHERUBS

STEWART & SALLY WALTON

PHOTOGRAPHY BY GRAHAM RAE

LORENZ BOOKS
LONDON • NEW YORK • SYDNEY • BATH

CONTENTS

$\mathcal{I}$NTRODUCTION

EVERY NOW AND THEN there is a breakthrough in interior decorating –
something suddenly captures the imagination. Stamping is definitely
one such breakthrough and it is all the more popular as it needs neither
specialist knowledge nor lots of money.

All you need is a stamp and some colour and you can make a start. The
idea comes from the office rubber stamp and it uses the same principle.

You can use stamps with a stamp pad, but a small foam roller gives a
better effect. The stamp can be coated with ordinary household paint –
this makes stamping a fairly inexpensive option, and gives you a wide
range of colours to choose from.

There are stamping projects in this book ranging from printing your
own T-shirt to creating a stylish but restful new look for your bedroom.

Each one is illustrated with clear step-by-step photographs and
instructions. You are bound to progress on to your own projects once
you've tried these suggestions because stamping really is so easy. The
added bonus is that you need very little equipment and there's hardly
any clearing up to do afterwards – what could be better?

This book focuses on cherubs – those chubby angel babies that have
their origins in ancient history. Cupid, the son of the Goddess of Love,
Venus, was a bundle of mischief whose magical arrows caused people to
fall hopelessly in love with each other. The great painters and sculptors
of the Italian Renaissance filled their clouds with cherubs, often using
the cherubs' facial expressions to add a touch of frivolity to their serious
works of art. Even today, we still call upon the powers of Cupid to help
us in our affairs of the heart.

The colours you choose for the cherub designs can result in many
different effects: natural creams and browns will give them a sculptural
quality, black creates a formal silhouette, while silver and gold have a
more romantic feeling. Whether you use the cherub and swag stamps to
create a Victorian-style frieze, a vase for your Valentine or to announce
the Christening of a newborn baby, their charm will work its magic.

BASIC APPLICATION TECHNIQUES

Stamping is a simple and direct way of making a print. The variations, such as they are, come from the way in which the stamp is inked and the type of surface to which it is applied. The stamps used in the projects were inked with a foam roller which is easy to do and gives reliable results, but each application technique has its own character. It is a good idea to experiment and find the method and effect that you most prefer.

INKING WITH A BRUSH
The advantage of this technique is that you can see where the colour has been applied. This method is quite time-consuming, so use it for smaller projects. It is ideal for inking an intricate stamp with more than one colour.

INKING WITH A FOAM ROLLER
This is the best method for stamping large areas, such as walls. The stamp is evenly inked and you can see where the colour has been applied. Variations in the strength of printing can be achieved by only re-inking the stamp after several printings.

INKING ON A STAMP PAD
This is the traditional way to ink rubber stamps, which are less porous than foam stamps. The method suits small projects, particularly those involving printing on paper. Stamp pads are more expensive to use than paint but are less messy, and will produce very crisp prints.

INKING BY DIPPING IN PAINT
Spread a thin layer of paint on to a flat plate and dip the stamp into it. This is the quickest way of stamping large decorating projects. As you cannot see how much paint the stamp is picking up, you will need to experiment.

INKING WITH FABRIC PAINT
Spread a thin layer of fabric paint on to a flat plate and dip the stamp into it. Fabric paints are quite sticky and any excess paint is likely to be taken up in the fabric rather than to spread around the edges. Fabric paint can also be applied by brush or foam roller, and is available with integral applicators from specialist outlets.

INKING WITH SEVERAL COLOURS
A brush is the preferred option when using more than one colour on a stamp. It allows greater accuracy than a foam roller because you can see exactly where you are putting the colour. Two-colour stamping is very effective for giving a shadow effect or a decorative pattern.

SURFACE APPLICATIONS

The surface on to which you stamp your design will greatly influence the finished effect.
Below are just some of the effects which can be achieved.

STAMPING ON ROUGH PLASTER

You can roughen your walls before stamping by mixing filler to a fairly loose consistency and spreading it randomly on the wall. When dry, roughen with coarse sandpaper, using random strokes.

STAMPING ON SMOOTH PLASTER OR LINING PAPER

Ink the stamp with a small foam roller for the crispest print. You can create perfect repeats by re-inking with every print, whereas making several prints between inkings varies the strength of the prints and is more in keeping with hand-printing.

STAMPING ON WOOD

Rub down the surface of any wood to give the paint a better "key" to adhere to. Some woods are very porous and absorb paint, but you can intensify the colour by over-printing later. Wood looks best lightly stamped so that the grain shows through. Seal your design with clear matt varnish.

STAMPING ON GLASS

Wash glass in hot water and detergent to remove any dirt or grease and dry thoroughly. It is best to stamp on glass for non-food uses, such as vases or sun-catchers. Ink the stamp with a foam roller and practise on a spare sheet of glass. As glass has a slippery, non-porous surface, you need to apply the stamp with a direct on/off movement. Each print will have a slightly different character, and the glass's transparency allows the pattern to be viewed from all sides.

STAMPING ON TILES

Wash and dry glazed tiles thoroughly before stamping. If the tiles are already on the wall, avoid stamping in areas which require a lot of cleaning. The paint will only withstand a gentle wipe with a damp cloth. Loose tiles can be baked to add strength and permanence to the paint. Read the paint manufacturer's instructions (and disclaimers!) before you do this. Ink the stamp with a small foam roller and apply with a direct on/off movement.

STAMPING ON FABRIC

As a rule, natural fabrics are the most absorbent, but to judge the stamped effect, experiment on a small sample. Fabric paints come in a range of colours, but to obtain the subtler shades you may need to combine the primaries and black and white. Always place a sheet of card behind the fabric to protect your work surface. Apply the fabric paint with a foam roller, brush or by dipping. You will need more paint than for a wall, as fabric absorbs the paint more efficiently.

PAINT EFFECTS

Once you have mastered the basics of stamp decorating, there are other techniques that you can use to enrich the patterns and add variety. Stamped patterns can be glazed over, rubbed back or over-printed to inject subtle or dramatic character changes.

STAMPING EMULSION ON PLASTER, DISTRESSED WITH TINTED VARNISH

The stamped pattern will already have picked up the irregularities of the wall surface and, if you re-ink after several prints, some prints will look more faded than others. To give the appearance of old hand-blocked wallpaper, paint over the whole surface with a ready-mixed antiquing varnish. You can also add colour to a varnish, but never mix a water-based product with a spirit-based one.

STAMPING EMULSION ON PLASTER, COLOURED WITH TINTED VARNISH

If the paint has dried to a brighter or duller shade than you had hoped for, you can apply a coat of coloured varnish. It is possible to buy ready-mixed colour-tinted varnish or you can add colour to a clear varnish base. A blue tint will change a red into purple, a red will change yellow into orange, and so on. The colour changes are gentle because the background changes at the same time.

STAMPING WITH WALLPAPER PASTE, PVA GLUE AND WATERCOLOUR PAINT

Mix three parts pre-mixed wallpaper paste with one part PVA glue and add watercolours. These come ready-mixed in bottles with integral droppers. The colours are intense so you may only need a few drops. The combination gives a sticky substance which the stamp picks up well and which clings to the wall without drips. The PVA glue dries clear to give a bright, glazed finish.

STAMPING WITH A MIXTURE OF WALLPAPER PASTE AND EMULSION

Mix up some wallpaper paste and add one part to two parts emulsion. This mixture makes a thicker print that is less opaque than the usual emulsion version. It also has a glazed surface that picks up the light.

STAMPING EMULSION ON PLASTER, WITH A SHADOW EFFECT

Applying even pressure gives a flat, regular print. By pressing down more firmly on one side of the stamp you can create a shadow effect on one edge. This is most effective if you repeat the procedure, placing the emphasis on the same side each time.

STAMPING A DROPPED SHADOW EFFECT

To make a pattern appear three-dimensional, stamp each pattern twice. Make the first print in a dark colour that shows up well against a mid-tone background. For the second print, move the stamp slightly to one side and use a lighter colour.

DESIGNING WITH STAMPS

To design the pattern of stamps, you need to find a compromise between printing totally at random and measuring precisely to achieve a machine-printed regularity. To do this, you can use the stamp block itself to give you a means of measuring your pattern, or try strips of paper, squares of card and lengths of string. Try using a stamp pad on scrap paper to plan your design but always wash and dry the stamp before proceeding to the main event.

USING PAPER CUT-OUTS
The easiest way to plan your design is to stamp and cut out as many pattern elements as you need and use them to mark the position of your finished stamped prints.

CREATING A REPEAT PATTERN
Use a strip of paper as a measuring device for repeat patterns. Cut the strip the length of one row of the pattern. Use the stamp block to mark where each print will go, with equal spaces in between. You could mark up a vertical strip, too. Position the horizontal strip against this as you print.

USING A PAPER SPACING DEVICE
This method is very simple. Decide on the distance between prints and cut a strip of paper to that size. Each time you stamp, place the strip against the edge of the previous print and line up the edge of the block with the other side of the strip. Use a longer strip to measure the distance required.

CREATING AN IRREGULAR PATTERN
If your design doesn't fit into a regular grid, plan the pattern first on paper. Cut out paper shapes to represent the spaces and use these to position the finished pattern. Alternatively, raise a motif above the previous one by stamping above a strip of card positioned on the baseline.

DEVISING A LARGER MOTIF
Use the stamps in groups to make up a larger design. Try stamping four together in a block, or partially overlapping an edge so that only a section of the stamp is shown. Use the stamps upside down, back to back and rotated in different ways. Experiment on scrap paper first.

USING A PLUMBLINE
Attach a plumbline at ceiling height to hang down the wall. Hold a card square behind the plumbline so that the string cuts through two opposite corners. Mark all four points, then move the card square down. Continue in this way to make a grid for stamping a regular pattern.

CHERUB BEDROOM

This bedroom has been given a complete cherubic transformation but the use of a subtle, natural colour scheme has prevented the effect from being overwhelming. Earthy colours harmonize naturally to produce a restful atmosphere. The three-dimensional effect on the walls is achieved by stamping first in a darker shade and then slightly off-register in a lighter colour. The cherubs seem to float free of the wall surface, which is most fitting for these little winged beings. The muslin drapes hang from a semi-circular shelf above the bed to make a soft frame around the pillows. The cherubs are stamped in cream fabric paint to create a very delicate pattern.

YOU WILL NEED
plumbline
25 x 25cm/10 x 10in card
pencil
emulsion paint in terracotta and cream
plates
foam rollers
cherub and swag stamps
10m/11yd unbleached muslin
iron
scissors
needle and matching sewing thread
newspaper
strip of cardboard
pen
ruler
fabric paint in cream and terracotta
semicircular wooden shelf and
wall fixtures
staple gun and staples
two rough silk cushion covers
backing card
black stamp pad
scrap paper
tassels
two cushion pads
vase
clean cloth
terracotta acrylic enamel paint

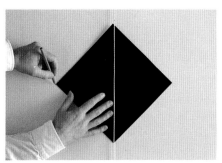

1 Attach a plumbline at ceiling height, just in from one corner. Hold the card square against the wall so that the string cuts through the top and bottom corners. Mark all the corner points in pencil. Move the card to continue marking a grid for stamping.

2 Spread some terracotta emulsion paint on to a plate and run a roller through it until it is evenly coated. Use it to ink the first cherub stamp and make a print with the base of the stamp resting on one of the pencil marks. Cover the wall with cherubs, re-inking the stamp as necessary.

3 Clean and dry the stamp, then re-ink it with cream emulsion. Position the stamp slightly to the right and just above each terracotta cherub print to achieve a three-dimensional effect.

4 To make the drapes, wash and iron the muslin before use, then cut it into two 5m/5½yd pieces and hem the ends. Cover a table with newspaper and lay the muslin flat.

5 Make a spacer from a long strip of cardboard, by ruling lines across the strip at regular intervals. Spread some cream fabric paint on to a plate and run a roller through it until it is evenly coated. Ink the first cherub stamp and print a row across the muslin above alternate marks on the spacer.

6 Print the second row of cherubs to fall between those in the first row. Use the paper strip to maintain an even distance between the rows. Move the fabric down and continue stamping to cover the whole length. Stamp the second drape in the same way. Follow the manufacturer's instructions to fix the fabric paint with an iron.

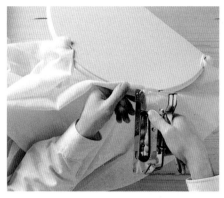

7 Staple the drapes to the shelf so that they meet at the front. Attach the edges first, then pleat the muslin and staple each fold to the shelf. Insert the staples vertically so that they are hidden in the folds. Fix the shelf to the wall, centrally above the bed and at picture rail height. Allow the drapes to fall on either side of the bed and cascade on to the floor.

8 To make the cushions, insert the backing card inside the cushion covers and lay on a flat surface.

9 Use the stamp pad to print both cherub stamps on scrap paper. Arrange them on the cushion cover to plan your design.

10 Spread some terracotta fabric paint on to a plate and run a roller through it until it is evenly coated. Ink the cherub stamps and print on to the fabric, removing each paper motif as you stamp in its place. Follow the manufacturer's instructions to fix the fabric paint with an iron.

11 Sew tassels on to the corners of the cushion covers and insert the cushion pads.

12 To stamp the vase, first wash it in hot water and detergent, then wipe dry with a clean cloth to ensure that there is no grease on the surface.

13 Spread some terracotta acrylic enamel paint on to a plate. Run a roller through it until it is evenly coated and ink the swag stamp.

14 Stamp swags around the vase. Remove the stamp directly and take care that it does not slide on the smooth surface and smudge the print. If you do make a mistake, wipe off the paint with a clean cloth and start again. Follow the manufacturer's instructions to "fire" the vase in a domestic oven.

WEDDING ALBUM COVER

Custom-made wedding photograph albums are never as special as one you make yourself. For most of us, a wedding is the only time we are photographed professionally looking our very best, so the presentation should do the pictures justice. The album should have a solid spine, so don't choose the spiral-bound type. Visit a specialist paper dealer and discover the wonderful range of textured papers. The paper is stamped with gold size and gold leaf is laid on to it to create gleaming golden cherubs and swags. Initials or the date of the wedding add the finishing touch.

YOU WILL NEED
white textured paper
large photograph album with a solid spine
scissors or scalpel
double-sided sticky tape
cherub and swag stamps
black stamp pad
scrap paper
gold size
plate
foam roller
gold transfer leaf
soft-bristled paintbrush
gold transfer letters or fine artist's brush

1 Lay the opened album on the sheet of paper and trim the paper to size. Allow a border round the edges to fold over the paper inside the cover. Cover the album with the paper, sticking down the overlaps on the inside of the cover.

2 Stamp several cherubs and swags on scrap paper and cut them out. Lay them out on the album cover with any initials or dates to plan your design. When you are happy with the design, use the paper cut-outs as a guide for positioning the stamps.

3 Spread some gold size on to a plate and run the roller through it until it is evenly coated. Ink the stamps with size and stamp the design on the album cover. Leave to dry for the time recommended by the manufacturer until the size becomes tacky.

4 Lay sheets of gold leaf on to the size and burnish with a soft brush.

5 Brush away any excess gold leaf still clinging to the paper. Add initials and the date, if required, using gold transfer letters or paint them freehand in size and gild as before.

BLISSFUL BATHROOM

Sea-greens and turquoise-blues are ideal for the watery environment of a bathroom and the floaty mood can be enhanced by the addition of coloured muslin drapes or glass jars filled with foam bath. The walls are first colourwashed and then a cherub border is stamped in sea-green. When the border has dried, a tinted varnish is brushed on to protect it and add another watery dimension. The chair back is stamped in emulsion paint and then varnished in a different shade. The plain wooden cupboard is stamped with cherubs and rubbed back to give it an aged look.

YOU WILL NEED
emulsion paint in turquoise, cream, sea-green and pale blue
wallpaper paste, mixed according to the manufacturer's instructions
household paintbrushes
plates
foam rollers
cherub and swag stamps
pencil (optional)
spirit level (optional)
small strip of card
clear water-based varnish and brush
sepia artist's watercolour
wooden kitchen chair with broad back-rest
fine artist's paintbrush
wire wool
small wooden hall cupboard
fine-grade sandpaper
clean cloth

1 Paint the walls turquoise. Mix one part cream emulsion with one part wallpaper paste and four parts water. Using random brush-strokes, paint the walls. Spread some sea-green emulsion on to a plate and run a roller through it. Ink the first cherub stamp.

2 Rest the base of the stamp block on the top edge of the rail or tiles, or use a pencil and spirit level to mark a line as a guide. Print a row of cherubs, alternating the two stamps and using a card strip to space the border. Tint the varnish with artist's watercolour and brush it over the whole wall.

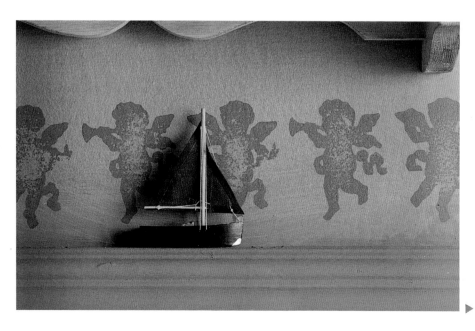

3 To stamp the chair, first paint it sea-green and leave to dry. Spread some turquoise emulsion paint on to a plate and mix in some cream paint to lighten the shade. Run a roller through the paint until it is evenly coated. Ink the swag stamp and print a swag in the centre of the chair back.

4 Lighten the sea-green paint further with cream and add hand-painted detail to the stamped swag with a fine paintbrush. Leave to dry. Rub back the paint with wire wool to simulate natural wear and tear. Apply a coat of clear varnish.

5 To stamp the cupboard, first paint it in pale blue emulsion paint. Before it has dried, rub back the paint with a clean cloth so that the pale blue colour stays in the grain, but much of the wood is revealed.

6 Rub back the paint with fine-grade sandpaper to reveal some more of the wood underneath.

7 Spread some sea-green emulsion paint on to a plate and run the roller through it until it is evenly coated. Ink both cherub stamps and make two prints on the door panel. Leave to dry.

8 Lightly rub back the cherub stamps with a cloth to give an antique look.

ANGEL T-SHIRTS

Fabric paints are very easy to use, come in a wide range of colours and can be fixed with a hot iron to make them washable and permanent. The cherubs can be used in many ways, including the funky colour combinations chosen here. Strong contrasts, complimentary shades or dayglo colours will all give the cherub a new image. By overprinting the cherubs slightly off-register in a second colour, you can add a three-dimensional look, too. Wash and iron the T-shirt before printing to remove any glazes that may block the absorption of the fabric paint.

YOU WILL NEED
plain-coloured T-shirts
backing card
cherub and swag stamps
black stamp pad
scrap paper
scissors
fabric paint in various colours
plate
foam roller
ruler (optional)
iron

1 Lay a T-shirt on a flat surface and insert the backing card to prevent the paint from passing through to the other side.

2 Stamp several cherubs or cherubs and swags on scrap paper. Cut them out and arrange them on the T-shirt to plan your design.

3 Spread some fabric paint on to a plate and run the roller through it until it is evenly coated. Ink the cherub stamp and print the pattern, removing each paper motif and stamping a cherub in its place. Re-ink the stamp after each print and press down firmly with the stamp to allow the fabric paint to penetrate the fabric.

4 Use a ruler to help align the pattern if necessary. Experiment with other patterns and colours. Follow the paint manufacturer's instructions to fix the design with an iron.

HEAVENLY HALLWAY

The cherubs are stamped in silhouette on this hallway wall, framed in medallions of pale yellow on a dove-grey background. The yellow medallions are stencilled on to the grey background and the combination of colours softens the potentially hard-edged dark silhouettes. The stencil can be cut from card or transparent mylar and the paint is applied with the same roller that is used for inking the stamps. The cherubic theme is extended to the painted wooden key box and the lampshade.

YOU WILL NEED
emulsion paint in dove-grey, pale yellow
and charcoal-grey
household paintbrushes
plumbline
25 x 25cm/10 x 10in card
pencil
ruler
stencil card
scalpel or craft knife
cutting mat
plates
foam rollers
cherub and swag stamps
lidded wooden box
fine-grade sandpaper
cloth
burnt-umber artist's oil colour
cream fabric lampshade and ceramic
lamp base
black stamp pad
scrap paper
scissors
masking tape

1 Paint the wall dove-grey and leave to dry. Attach a plumbline at ceiling height, just in from one corner. Hold the card square against the wall so that the string cuts through the top and bottom corners. Mark all the corner points in pencil. Move the card and continue marking the wall to make a grid for the stamps.

2 Use a pencil and ruler to draw the medallion shape on a sheet of stencil card. Carefully cut out the stencil using a scalpel or craft knife on a cutting mat. Spread yellow emulsion paint on to a plate and run the roller through it until it is evenly coated.

3 Position the stencil on one of the pencil marks and use the paint-covered roller to stencil the medallion shape. Paint all the medallions in this way, positioning the stencil in the same place on each pencil mark.

4 Ink the first cherub stamp with charcoal-grey paint and make a print inside each medallion.

5 Paint the wooden box pale yellow, inside and out, and leave to dry.

6 Spread some charcoal-grey paint on to a plate and run a roller through it until it is evenly coated. Ink the second cherub stamp and make a print in the centre of the box lid. Print the swag stamp directly beneath the cherub.

7 Measure the sides of the box to determine the number of swag prints that will fit comfortably in a row. Mark the positions in pencil or judge by eye to add swags around the sides of the box. Leave to dry.

8 Rub the corners and edges of the box with fine-grade sandpaper. Rub the prints in places to add a faded, aged look. Use a cloth to rub burnt-umber artist's oil colour on to the whole box, to give an antique appearance.

9 For the lampshade, stamp several swags on scrap paper and cut them out. Arrange the cut-outs on the lampshade to plan your design. Hold each piece in place with a small piece of masking tape.

10 Spread some dove-grey paint on to a plate and run a roller through it until it is evenly coated. Ink the swag stamp and print swags around the top of the lampshade, removing each paper motif before you stamp in its place.

11 Continue stamping around the base of the shade in the same way, removing each paper motif in turn.

12 Stamp swags around the lamp base to complete the co-ordinated look. Judge the positioning by eye or use paper motifs as before.

CHERUB SHOPPING BAG

Large canvas shopping bags with shoulder straps are both fashionable and useful. They come in a range of plain colours that seem to cry out to be given an individual touch. Stamping works well on canvas and you can choose from fabric paint, acrylics or household emulsion. Bear in mind that you will not be able to wash the bag if you use emulsion or acrylic, while fabric paint can be fixed with an iron to make it permanent and washable.

YOU WILL NEED
blue canvas shopping bag
backing card
cherub and swag stamps
black stamp pad
scrap paper
scissors
emulsion, acrylic or fabric paint in white
and pale blue
plate
foam roller
iron (optional)

1 Lay the bag on a flat surface and insert the backing card to prevent the paint from passing through to the other side.

2 Make several cherub and swag prints on scrap paper. Cut them out and arrange them on the bag to plan your design.

3 Spread some white paint on to the plate and run the roller through it until it is evenly coated. Ink the cherub and swag stamps and print the pattern, removing each paper motif and stamping in its place. Leave to dry, then ink the edges of the stamps with pale blue paint. Over-print the white design to create a shadow effect. If using fabric paint, follow the paint manufacturer's instructions to fix the design with an iron.

CUPID MUGS

Considering the range of mugs produced, it can be extraordinarily difficult to find one that has the shape, colour and pattern that you like. This project mixes and matches the colours of the mugs and patterns, while sticking to the same simple shape. Mugs can be successfully stamped with acrylic enamel paints and "fired" in a domestic oven to make the design permanent. Follow the manufacturer's instructions and the paint will then withstand the hottest washing-up water.

YOU WILL NEED
four mugs in different colours
acrylic enamel paints in the same four
colours (or as close as possible)
four plates
foam roller
cherub stamps

1 Wash the mugs in hot water and detergent and dry thoroughly. Spread one colour of acrylic enamel paint on to each of the plates. Decide which colour to stamp on each mug.

2 Run the roller through one of the colours until it is evenly coated and use it to ink the stamp. Stamp the cherub on the first mug, removing the stamp directly to prevent it from sliding on the smooth surface.

3 Wash and dry the roller and stamp, then re-ink and stamp the second mug. Stamp all four mugs in this way, using both cherub stamps. Follow the manufacturer's instructions to "fire" the mugs in a domestic oven to make the design permanent.

CHRISTENING PARTY

The gift paper, cards and table setting of this project will all help to make a traditional christening or naming day party an unforgettable occasion. Use the cherubs to announce the baby's birth and then herald the start of the celebrations. Buy a good-quality white paper for the cards. Some papers are deckle-edged, while others are textured. The choice is a personal one and a textured surface will give interesting stamped effects, so experiment on samples of paper. Set off the hand-printed wrapping paper with white satin ribbons and bows.

YOU WILL NEED
large white tablecloth or sheet
backing card
fabric paint in bottle-green and silver
plates
foam rollers
swag and cherub stamps
iron
paper table napkins in white and bottle-green
acrylic paint in bottle-green, white and blue-grey
white note-paper
scissors
ruler
pencil
water-based size
silver transfer leaf
fine wire wool
silver wrapping paper
newspaper
black stamp pad
scrap paper
small strip of card

1 Lay the tablecloth or sheet on a table. Ink the swag stamp with bottle-green fabric paint and print across one corner of the cloth, so that the tassels are about 2.5cm/1in from the edges. Stamp swags all around the edge of the cloth to create a scalloped effect.

2 Spread some silver fabric paint on to a plate and run a roller through it until it is evenly coated. Ink both cherub stamps and, alternating the two designs, make a print above every other swag.

3 Continue to stamp a widely spaced cherub pattern in the centre of the cloth, alternating both stamps and rotating the direction of the prints. Follow the manufacturer's instructions to fix the paint with an iron.

4 For the napkins, spread some green acrylic paint on to a plate and run a roller through it until it is evenly coated. Ink the cherub stamps and make one print on each white table napkin.

5 Spread some white acrylic paint on to a plate. Use a roller to ink the cherub stamps. Stamp a white cherub on each green napkin.

6 To make the cards, cut and fold the paper to the required size, which should be at least 14 x 11.5cm/5½ x 4½in. Draw pencil lines on the back of the stamp block to mark the mid-points on each side to help you position the stamp accurately each time. Spread some blue-grey acrylic paint on to a plate and run a roller through it until it is evenly coated. Ink the stamp and print cherubs on all the cards. Leave to dry.

7 Spread water-based size on to a plate and run a roller through it until it is evenly coated. Ink the cherub stamps with size and overprint the blue-grey prints. Leave to dry for the time recommended by the manufacturer until the size becomes tacky. Lay sheets of silver leaf on to the size and burnish the backing paper with a soft cloth.

8 Remove the backing paper and use wire wool to rub away any excess silver leaf still clinging to the paper.

9 To make the wrapping paper, lay the silver paper on some newspaper on a flat surface. Stamp several cherubs and swags on scrap paper and cut them out. Arrange the paper motifs on the silver paper to plan your design. Cut a card strip as a guide to the spacing between the motifs.

10 Spread some bottle-green acrylic paint on to a plate and run a roller through it until it is evenly coated. Ink the cherub stamp and print cherubs on the silver paper. Use the card strip to space the stamps.

11 Ink the swag stamp with white paint and print the linking swags between the cherubs.

VALENTINE VASE

Present a dozen red roses in this beautiful stamped vase and you won't need Cupid's arrow to get your point across! There are a number of different types of glass paint on the market, but this vase is stamped with acrylic enamels, which work on glazed ceramics as well. The cupid is first stamped in white, then painted over with a mottled silver, which is achieved by dabbing paint on with a brush. A heart stencil is cut from card and used in combination with the cherub to complete the romantic Valentine theme.

YOU WILL NEED
pencil
stencil card or plastic
scalpel or craft knife
cutting mat
plain glass vase
acrylic enamel paint in red, cream and white
plate
foam roller
stencil brush (optional)
cherub stamp
artist's paintbrush

1 Draw a heart shape on to a small piece of stencil card or plastic. Cut out the stencil with a scalpel or craft knife on a cutting mat.

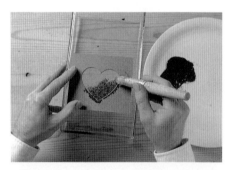

2 Position the heart stencil on the vase. Use red acrylic enamel paint and either the foam roller or the stencil brush to stencil the heart.

3 Spread some cream acrylic enamel paint on to a plate and run the roller through it until it is evenly coated. Ink the cherub stamp and make a print above the heart. Remove the stamp directly to prevent it from sliding. Use the artist's paintbrush to stipple a mottled coating of white over the cherub. Do not cover the whole print.

ANGELIC TRAY

Ease the guilt caused by a late-night snack by serving it on this angelic tray decorated with chocolate swags. Wooden trays can often be found in charity or junk shops, usually coated with sticky-backed plastic or several layers of gloss paint. Rescue such a tray by giving it a good scrub and rubbing away all the paint with sandpaper before treating it to a new coat of paint. Then have fun embellishing it in chocolate colours.

YOU WILL NEED
emulsion paint in cream and
chocolate-brown
household paintbrush
black stamp pad
swag stamp
scrap paper
scissors
plate
foam roller
clear water-based varnish
and brush

1 Paint the tray cream and leave to dry. Use the stamp pad to print several swags on scrap paper and cut them out. Arrange the cut-outs on the tray to plan your design.

2 Spread some chocolate-brown paint on to a plate and run the roller through it. Ink the swag stamp and print the pattern, removing each paper motif to stamp in its place.

3 When dry, paint the sides of the tray brown inside and out, leaving the top of the rim cream. Leave to dry, then apply a coat of clear varnish.

First published in 1996 by Lorenz Books

© Anness Publishing Limited 1996

Lorenz Books is an imprint of Anness Publishing Limited
Boundary Row Studios
1 Boundary Row
London SE1 8HP

ISBN 1 85967 228 0

Distributed in Canada by Raincoast Books Distribution Limited

A CIP catalogue record for this book is available from the British Library

Publisher: Joanna Lorenz
Project Editor: Lindsay Porter
Designer: Bobbie Colgate Stone
Photographer: Graham Rae
Stylist: Fanny Ward

Printed and bound in Singapore

ACKNOWLEDGMENTS
The authors and publishers would like to thank Sacha Cohen, Josh George and Sarah Pullen for all their hard work in the studio

Paints supplied by Crown Paints, Crown Decorative Products Ltd, P.O. Box 37, Crown House, Hollins Road, Darwen, Lancashire BB3 0BG. Specialist paints supplied by Paint Magic, 79 Shepperton Road, Islington, London N1 3DF

BISON DELIGHTS

BISON DELIGHTS

middle eastern cuisine, western style

Habeeb Salloum

CPRC
PRESS

Printed and bound in Canada at Friesens.

Cover and text design by Duncan Campbell, CPRC Press.
Edited by Donna Grant, CPRC Press.

Photos: All by iStockphoto, except pp. 27, 28, 30, 58, 73, 100, 111 by Fotolia;
p. 152 by Habeeb Salloum; and pp. 4, 8, 22, 35, 55, 71, 80, 89, 95, 119, and 146
by Carolyn Pihach Photography, with art direction and food styling by Duncan Campbell.

Library and Archives Canada Cataloguing in Publication

Salloum, Habeeb, 1924—
Bison delights : Middle Eastern cuisine, western style / Habeeb Salloum.

(TBS ; 26)
Includes bibliographical references and index.
ISBN 978-0-88977-215-1

1. Cookery (Buffalo meat). 2. Cookery, Middle Eastern.
I. Title. II. Series: TBS 26

TX749.5.B84S25 2010   641.6'6292   C2009-906829-X

CANADIAN PLAINS RESEARCH CENTER
University of Regina
Regina, Saskatchewan
Canada, S4S 0A2
tel: (306) 585-4758
fax: (306) 585-4699
e-mail: canadian.plains@uregina.ca
web: www.cprc.uregina.ca
www.cprcpress.ca

FSC
Mixed Sources
Cert no. SW-COC-001271
© 1996 FSC

We acknowledge the financial support of the Government of Canada through the Book
Publishing Industry Development Program (BPIDP) for our publishing activities. We also
acknowledge the support of the Canada Council for the Arts for our publishing program.

Canadian Patrimoine
Heritage canadien

Canada Council Conseil des Arts
for the Arts du Canada

acknowledgements

I wish especially to thank my daughters Muna Salloum and Leila Salloum Elias for their valuable advice about the recipes included in this book, for providing the historical background to some of the foods and for help in testing and tasting a number of the recipes. Thanks to members of the Canadian Plains Research Center (CPRC) for their commitment and dedication to the publication process. Specifically, I want to thank Brian Mlazgar, CPRC Publications Manager, for encouraging me to write this modest work; Donna Grant, Senior Editor, for her expert advice and editorial work; and Duncan Campbell, CPRC Art and Design Coordinator, for the beautiful book and cover design. In addition, my gratitude goes out to those authors whose books provided interesting material, which I included in a number of my stories.

contents

For eons herds of bison roamed, lords of the prairie space,
Their life and actions barely hindered by the human race,
Then strangers with fire-spitting weapons came
To conquer the land and the majestic herds erase.

PREFACE

These few lines tell the sad tale of the North American bison, once the lifeblood of the indigenous peoples of North America. Like my parents, very few settlers who pioneered in southwestern Saskatchewan had any idea that the land they ploughed was once the domain of the bison.

As children, my brother and I would roam the unploughed valleys of the grasslands and often find skulls, which we were later to learn were those of bison, or "buffalo," as they were commonly called at the time. During my youth, I never saw a bison except in pictures and, later, only in zoos. Yet, I vividly remember strolling across our pasture land, never touched by the plough, singing in the open spaces:

Oh, give me a home where the buffalo roam,
and the deer and the antelope play,
Where seldom is heard a discouraging word,
And the skies are not cloudy all day.

Today, I have no idea where I picked up this song—perhaps from one of my playmates in school. I had seen antelopes on our farm but never buffalo. Long before my time, the bison had been erased from the empty spaces through which I roamed.

I was therefore excited one summer day in 2008 as my guide from the Saskatchewan Department of Tourism and I made our way to Grasslands National Park—Canada's only virgin prairie. Located in southwestern Saskatchewan, the park happens to edge the land that was our family's homestead. Here, the prairie has been returned to its natural state. Here, I hoped to see a herd of bison.

In 2005 Parks Canada began to release bison into Grasslands National Park, onto land that had been home to thousands of bison until they were nearly wiped out more than a century ago by white hunters. As I stood gazing on the small bison herd that now roams this land, feeding on the natural grasses and other plants on which their ancestors thrived, I thought of the age when 70 million bison roamed the North American western plains. Before the advent of the Europeans, bison were so numerous that when the huge herds stampeded across the prairie they sounded like rolling thunder—hence their nickname, "thunder of the plains." On this day, I imagined hearing and feeling the thunder of a great bison herd as it stampeded over the open prairie grasslands.

The largest land animal indigenous to North America, the bison dominated the continent from the time of the ice age until settlers began to populate the prairies. For thousand of years, the indigenous peoples of the prairies relied on the bison for clothing, shelter, tools and food. But the arrival of Europeans nearly wiped out the bison population. Before the turn of the twentieth century, fewer than 1,000 were verified to have survived. For more information about the history of the bison and the indigenous people of the Plains, see the Selected Reading List on page 163.

Today, more than a century after their near-demise, the bison, once the mainstay of the Plains First Nations, has made a dramatic comeback. The irreversible loss of the bison was prevented by the work of but a few dedicated people: through the effort of indigenous people, ranchers and conservationists in both Canada and the United States over the past several decades, bison numbers have increased. The search for heart-healthy and gourmet meats has led to the commercial ranching of bison, and today, while some herds are found in parks, the majority are raised on farms or ranches across North America.

As I researched the history of the bison, always in the back of my mind were the prairies, where I grew up and where once herds of bison stretched as far as the eye could see. At times, I would get a strange feeling that, although as a youth I had never seen bison, they were yet a part of my life. When I saw them roaming free in Grasslands National Park during my last trip through southern Saskatchewan, it gave me a feeling of satisfaction. At last I had seen the bison, as it was when it was king of the prairies.

Later, when I cooked my bison dishes, their enticing aroma captured to some extent the mouth-watering aromas from my mother's farm kitchen when she cooked our tasty Middle Eastern foods, especially the lamb dishes. As the succulent odours from my bison dishes enveloped our small kitchen, I thought about what a great replacement bison was for lamb. Its aroma not only made me hungry, but also brought back memories of the prairies, where once the bison roamed the plains.

Like many meats, bison can be prepared in numerous ways. I hope that the recipes in this book, prepared in both the Middle Eastern and the North African Arab style of cooking, will inspire you to try this "rediscovered" historical Prairie staple now considered among the world's finest gourmet delicacies.

Bison Meat—FOR FLAVOUR AND HEALTH

What the indigenous peoples of North America had known for hundreds of years is again being discovered today. Bison meat is one of the prime meats that humans can consume. The meat of grass-fed bison has a distinct, natural flavour with a slightly sweeter and richer taste than beef. It has no "gamey" or wild taste, and its regular users claim that bison meat is far superior to most store-bought beef or other meats.

In the words of one of my relatives in Saskatchewan: "Think of the most tender beef you've ever eaten, then try bison tenderloin! You'll be surprised at its tenderness and tastiness!"

Once considered exotic, bison meat is now sought after by health-conscious consumers, who look on it as a natural food product. Bison are raised with no growth stimulants, hormones or antibiotics, and bison meat is not preserved in nitrites or other preservatives. Some historians claim that, since bison was their main food, it is not surprising that the indigenous peoples of the Plains knew little of cancer, heart disease and heart attacks, with many living 85 to 90 years.

Below are some easy-to-reference facts and tips about bison nutrition, handling and cooking, followed by other interesting facts.

bison facts and tips

NUTRITION FACTS

* Bison meat is the only red meat that is non-allergenic.

* Bison meat has the highest percentage of protein of any meat tested—containing about 20 percent protein compared with 10 percent found in beef.

* Bison meat is rich in copper, iron, niacin, phosphorus, potassium, riboflavin, selenium, zinc, and vitamins B_6 and B_{12}.

* Bison meat is lower in cholesterol and contains fewer calories per serving (depending upon the cut of the meat) than beef, chicken (with skin), lamb, pork, veal, venison and sockeye salmon.

* Bison meat has 6 percent fat compared to 25–30 percent in beef. It is high in the good, unsaturated fats.

* The meat of bison raised on pasture grass is rich in omega-3 fatty acid, an important nutrient for reducing blood pressure, stimulating blood circulation, reducing the risk of heart attacks and reducing symptoms associated with rheumatoid arthritis.

* The American Heart Association recommends bison meat for a heart-healthy diet, due to its low fat and cholesterol content. The Mayo Clinic was one of the first to come out with the data in their *Mayo Clinic Nutrition Letter* of November 1989.

BASIC HANDLING TIPS

Keep bison meat in its package until ready to use. Freeze in its original packaging. If it is to be frozen for longer than 2 months, over-wrap the original packaging with plastic wrap. When frozen, ground bison meat will retain its best quality for 4 months, other cuts for 6 to 9 months.

Defrost frozen bison meat by slowly thawing in the refrigerator, by submersing in cold water without removing packaging or by defrosting in the microwave. Cook immediately. You may decide to defrost the meat during cooking. If so, allow one-third to one-half more cooking time, depending on the size of the cut.

Cooked bison meat should be eaten or frozen within 4 days.

BASIC COOKING TIPS

Since bison meat is very lean and lacks fat, it cooks faster than other red meats. If overcooked, it becomes dry and loses much of its taste. Bison should not be served "well done." Instead, cook burgers, roasts and steaks to "medium rare" for the perfect balance of juiciness and flavour.

When cooking bison, use a temperature about 50° F (10° C) lower than the regular temperature you would use for cooking the same cut of beef. For example, cook bison roasts at 275° F (135° C).

When roasting bison, add water to come about halfway up the roast, then cover and bake in a preheated oven at 275° F (135° C) for about 1 to 2 hours per pound.

When grilling ¼ to ⅓-pound (110g-150g) bison burgers, cook 3 minutes on each side, turning only once. Remember that, because the meat is so lean, the cooked burger will be the same size as it was before cooking.

Stir-frying small strips or cubes of meat in a wok is an excellent way to cook bison. Heat the oil only enough to sear the meat, then stir the meat quickly around the wok, just for a minute or two. Add the other ingredients and stir-fry for another minute or two. The short cooking time needed for stir-frying makes bison meat ideal for this method of cooking.

Bison meat can be cooked in a microwave the same as any other red meat; use a lower setting.

OTHER BISON FACTS

* Cuts of bison are the same as those of beef.

* Bison contains virtually no marbling. Due to this lack of marbling, bison meat is usually deep red.

* The low fat content of bison results in greater penetration of marinades and sauces and, thus, better flavour.

* Ground bison can be used in any recipe that calls for the use of ground beef. It is even better than beef when used in such dishes as chili con carne, casseroles, meatballs, lasagne, soup and spaghetti.

* For recipes that call for partially cooked or raw meat use rib-eye or tenderloin cuts—they are the most tender cuts in bison meat.

* Of all the bison steaks, filet mignon, cut from the centre of the tenderloin, is the juiciest and most flavourful.

* Bison is a dense type of meat that tends to satisfy the diner more with less.

* The best meat comes from animals slaughtered between the ages of 18 months and 2½ years. If meat from bison older than 3 years is being used, allow more cooking time, especially when it comes to shoulder meat.

* Bison meat is more expensive than beef because it is less common, the breeding stock is more expensive and the meat is more expensive to produce. In the markets, it falls into the gourmet or specialty meat category. However, price should not be your only consideration when choosing meat; remember that bison meat has more protein and nutrients with fewer calories and less fat than other meats.

* The Canadian Bison Association (CBA), with some 850 members throughout Canada, has been a leading force in the restoration of the bison. It now serves over 1,800 bison producers on individual farms across the country. About 40 percent of these are in Saskatchewan.

* There are a number of advantages to raising bison over raising other animals for their meat: fewer illnesses and thus little or no veterinarian care, no need to be milked or grained, literally no calving problems, few death losses due to superior bison hardiness and a long reproductive life. ❧

accompaniments

I n Arab cuisine, every stew and many other dishes are served along with cooked rice, burghul, or, in North Africa, couscous. Following are the basic preparation instructions for these staple accompaniment dishes. You may also replace these with mashed or fried potatoes. ❧

Ruzz Mufalfal —BASIC RICE

Serves 4 to 6

This recipe of cooked rice is a simple dish to prepare.

4 Tbsp / 60 ml	butter
1 cup / 250 ml	rice, rinsed
2 cups / 500 ml	boiling water
½ tsp / 2 ml	salt

Melt butter in a frying pan, then stir-fry rice for two minutes. Add water and salt, then bring to a boil. Turn heat to medium-low, then cover and cook for 12 minutes. Stir, then re-cover. Turn off heat and allow to cook in its own steam for 30 minutes.

Basic Couscous

Serves 8 to 10 as a side dish

The name couscous could possibly be derived from the Arabic *kaskasa* (to pound small) or from *kiskis*, a perforated earthenware steamer pot, from which we get the word *couscousiére*. In Morocco, it has various names—*kusksi, kuskus, siksu* and *sikuk*; in Algeria, it is called *ta'am*; in Tunisia, *kouski*; in Sicily, *cuscusu*; in Senegal, *keskes*; in Brazil, where the art of making couscous was introduced by West African slaves, it is made with cornmeal, fish or other meat, and called *cuzcuz*.

Each of these countries prepares their couscous a little differently. The Moroccans gently blend numerous spices to concoct delightful creations; the Algerians often include sausages among the ingredients; Tunisian couscous is hot and wholesome; Sicilian couscous is made like a soup; West African couscous is made with sorghum; and the Brazilian version, with its cornmeal, is unique. In all other parts of the world, the preparation of couscous, in the main, follows the Moroccan pattern and, with the exception of France, where it has become a national dish, it is most commonly offered in restaurants operated by Moroccan expatriates.

2 cups / 500 ml	water
1 Tbsp / 15 ml	butter
½ tsp / 2 ml	salt
2 cups / 500 ml	couscous

Place water, butter and salt in a saucepan and bring to a boil. Stir in couscous, then remove from heat and cover. Let stand for 5 minutes. Fluff the couscous with a fork, then serve with stews, or stir in honey while still hot to make a dessert; or simply buy prepared couscous and follow package instructions.

Burghul Mufalfal —BASIC BURGHUL

Serves 4

In the last few years vegetarians and other health-conscious people have become convinced that burghul—otherwise known as bulgar, bulgor, bulgur and bulgourl—is an excellent health food. Research and experience have proven that this cereal has very few equals in food value. The cooking of the wheat preserves most of the nutrients, even when some of the bran is removed after the grain is crushed. The calcium, carbohydrates, iron, phosphorous, potassium, vitamin B, and protein content are almost all retained. These are not lost even when burghul is stored for a long period of time. The cereal can be kept for years without loss of food value or any other type of deterioration.

Unexcelled as a nourishing food, burghul has more food energy than cornmeal; more iron than rice; less fat than uncooked wheat; six times more calcium than cornmeal and three times more than rice; and more vitamins than barley, cornmeal or rice.

4 Tbsp / 60 ml	butter
½ cup / 125 ml	thin vermicelli, broken into 1-inch (2.5-cm) pieces
1 cup / 250 ml	coarse burghul, rinsed
2¼ cups / 560 ml	water
½ tsp / 2 ml	salt
¼ tsp / 1 ml	pepper

In a frying pan, melt the butter, then stir-fry vermicelli over medium heat until it just begins to turn brown. Stir in burghul, then stir-fry over medium heat for 2 minutes.

Stir in the remaining ingredients and bring to a boil, then cover and cook over medium-low heat for 20 minutes, stirring a number of times to make sure burghul does not stick to bottom of frying pan, then re-covering. Add a little more butter if needed. Shut off heat and stir, then re-cover and allow to cook in its own steam for a further 30 minutes. Serve as a side or main dish.

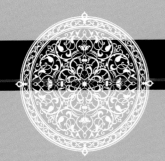

appetizers

When I decided to write a book consisting of stories and recipes relating to the North American bison, I doubted that I could create enough bison appetizers to warrant a chapter. Appetizers in the Middle East are, in the vast majority of cases, prepared from dairy products, pulses and vegetables. Consequently, it was somewhat of a challenge to create Middle East-inspired appetizers with bison meat as their basis. However, in the end, the bison meat recipes here are appetizing and tasty dishes that hosts in the Middle East would be proud to offer to important guests.

Called *mazzas* in Arabic, appetizers constitute one of the glories of Middle Eastern cuisine. These foreshadow the delights of the meal to come and are served on small dishes and typically in large numbers, depending on the formality and importance of the meal to follow. These appetizers range from the simple, such as small dishes of olives, various cheeses, sliced tomatoes, fresh broad beans or seasoned diced potatoes, to the more complex dishes like chickpea and eggplant purées or *taboula* and a number of meat tidbits.

Mazzas usually play an important role on the menu of every meal to which guests are invited. Served in restaurants and homes, these *mazzas* tempt unsuspecting and enchanted guests to eat too much before the main courses are presented. Not infrequently, guests are unable to eat the main course after sampling two or three dozen *mazzas* out of a total of perhaps one hundred or more. Moreover, the code of hospitality forbids warning the guests not to partake too much of the appetizers. Foreigners tend to eat so much of the delicious *mazzas* that they have no room left for the main meal. Even experienced visitors will have trouble confining themselves to a reasonable number of appetizers.

The dinner invitation to friends and colleagues always begins with this age-old practice. Usually, guests sit around a table covered with plates of *mazzas*. Everyone nibbles on whatever foods they fancy, chatting between mouthfuls. The *mazza* course of the meal often continues for hours. This delightful way to begin a meal—relaxed and conducive to socializing—has been established over millennia of civilized living in the Middle East.

Some historians believe that the Arabs carried the serving of these tidbits of foods to the Iberian peninsula during the 800 years that they were in that part of Europe. The Spanish tradition of gathering before a meal for a drink and for the sampling of endless appetizers, called *tapas*, matches the Arab custom. This pleasant precursor to an elaborate meal is found to a great extent only in the Middle East and in Spain.

Even in the homesteading years when food was scarce, my mother would not break with tradition. Whenever guests graced our kitchen table, *mazzas* were a must before serving the main course, for the *mazza* tradition worked hand-in-hand with hospitality and welcome. Small dishes of yogurt, small plates of greens infused with garlic, mashed chickpeas and parsley salads all served as humble *mazzas* for the honoured guests.

Today, an enormous variety of *mazzas*, from plain to sophisticated, are served at home or in public eating places throughout the Middle East and in many Middle Eastern restaurants in the Western world. It is hoped that our bison appetizers will in the future find their way to the tables of not only Middle Eastern restaurants, but also to many public eating places and homes in North America. ✾

Kufta Hilwa—APRICOT PATTIES

Makes about 48 small patties

The Chinese were the first to domesticate the apricot tree about 5,000 years ago. It became one of their favoured plants and, in the ensuing centuries, they came to believe that its fruit had special powers. In Chinese literature, we find that its blossoms were a symbol of love and seduction. From China, its cultivation spread to the nearby lands. Alexander the Great is credited with introducing the tree into Greece, and later its fruit became an important part of Roman cuisine. However, apricots never really took root in Europe until the Arabs brought them to the Iberian peninsula. Spain thereafter became the world's leading producer of this delicious fruit, and, through that country, almost all the European languages derived their name for apricots from the Arabic *al-barquq* (the apricot).

2 lbs / 907 g	ground bison
1 cup / 250 ml	chopped dried apricots
1	medium onion, chopped
4	cloves garlic, crushed
4 Tbsp / 60 ml	finely chopped coriander leaves
1 tsp / 5 ml	ground mustard
1 tsp / 5 ml	dried mint
1 tsp / 5 ml	sage
1 tsp / 5 ml	salt
½ tsp / 2 ml	pepper
⅛ tsp / ½ ml	cayenne
2	eggs

Place all ingredients in a food processor, then process until thoroughly mixed. Form into small patties approximately 2 to 3 inches (5 to 7.5 cm) in diameter, then place in a single layer on well-greased cookie sheets and bake uncovered in a 300° F (150° C) preheated oven for 1¼ hours or until the patties are done. Place on platters and serve as appetizers.

sfeehat jamus wa Rumman
—ARABIAN BISON–POMEGRANATE PIZZA

Serves about 9 as an entree

A Syrian/Lebanese-type pizza or pie, *sfeehah* can be made with meat, vegetables, or sweet, and can be open or filled. Its fame has spread as far as the Latin and Central American countries, where it is found in many restaurants. In Brazil, meat dishes of Arab origin are often made spicier than their Middle Eastern counterparts and are much sought after by the local population.

2 lbs / 907 g	frozen bread dough, thawed (or use homemade)
1 lb / 454 g	bison round steak, cut into very small pieces
1 cup / 250 ml	pomegranate seeds
2	medium onions, very finely chopped
4	cloves garlic, crushed
½ cup / 125 ml	finely chopped parsley
4 Tbsp / 60 ml	tomato paste
1 tsp / 5 ml	paprika
1 tsp / 5 ml	salt
½ tsp / 2 ml	pepper
½ tsp / 2 ml	ground coriander seeds
¼ tsp / 1 ml	cayenne
4 Tbsp / 60 ml	olive oil

Form dough into 36 small balls, then cover with a damp cloth and allow to rest for 2 hours.

In the meantime, make a filling by thoroughly combining the remaining ingredients, then divide filling into 36 parts and set aside.

With a rolling pin, roll dough balls into circles about 3 inches (7.5 cm) in diameter, then fold and pinch edges to make a raised rim. Spread one part of the filling inside the rim and pat down evenly with fingers, then continue until all the balls are finished.

Place on a well-greased cookie tray, then bake in a 300° F (150° C) preheated oven for 1 hour or until the rims of the circles turn light brown. Remove and brush edges with a little extra olive oil, then serve as an appetizer or as an entree.

malfoof mihshee or waraq ᶜinab mihshee
—CABBAGE ROLLS OR STUFFED GRAPE LEAVES

Serves about 8 as an entree

Meat-filled cabbage rolls are the most widely eaten of all the stuffed vegetables. Besides their traditional home in the Middle East and Eastern Europe, they are now well-known in Western Europe and North America. Carried to the western hemisphere by the millions of immigrants from the lands surrounding the eastern Mediterranean and the Balkans, today they are found on many restaurant menus in North American urban centres.

More exotic, yet akin to cabbage rolls, are the stuffed leaves of the grape. Very common in the eastern Mediterranean countries, they are a delicacy still to be discovered by the masses in the West. The epitome of stuffed foods to their great number of culinary fans, they are a very delicious gourmet treat.

For this recipe, a 1-pound jar of grape leaves can be substituted for the cabbage leaves. However, before use, the grape leaves must be thoroughly washed to remove all the salt in which they are preserved. Also, omit the 1 tsp (5 ml) of salt to be sprinkled over top of the stuffed cabbage leaves.

1	medium head cabbage (2 to 3 lbs/1 to 1.5 kg)	for stuffing	
1 tsp / 5 ml	salt	1 lb / 454 g	ground bison
8	cloves garlic, coarsely chopped	1 cup / 250 ml	rice, rinsed
½ cup / 125 ml	lemon juice	2 cups / 500 ml	stewed tomatoes
		4 Tbsp / 60 ml	melted butter
		4 Tbsp / 60 ml	finely chopped fresh mint
		2 Tbsp / 30 ml	finely chopped coriander leaves
		1 tsp / 5 ml	pepper
		1 tsp / 5 ml	cumin
		¾ tsp / 3 ml	allspice
		½ tsp / 2 ml	cinnamon
		⅛ tsp / ½ ml	cayenne
		1 tsp / 5 ml	salt

With a knife, score around the stem of the cabbage to loosen it. Place cabbage in a pot of boiling water, then cook for a few minutes to soften leaves. With a knife, loosen leaves from bottom. Trim thick ribs, then cut large leaves in half. (If inner leaves are not soft, boil again for few minutes.) Set leaves aside and reserve ribs.

Combine stuffing ingredients. Place some stuffing (amount depends on size of leaf) on wide end of cabbage leaf and roll, tucking in ends while rolling. Continue until all leaves are stuffed.

Cover bottom of a saucepan with trimmed cabbage ribs. Arrange rolls side by side in alternating layers, placing garlic pieces between rolls. Sprinkle 1 tsp (5 ml) salt over top, then add lemon juice. Cover with inverted plate, then add enough water barely to cover plate.

Bring to a boil, then cover and cook over medium-low heat for 1¼ hours or until meat and rice are done.

Serve hot as main course or as appetizers.

вαyd Malabas bi Lahm —EGGS ROLLED IN BISON

Serves 4

Popular in Iraq, this dish is not usually found in other places in the Middle East. The dish can also be served as an excellent entree. When prepared from bison meat, these will be a hit at any feast.

1 lb / 454 g	ground bison steak
1	medium onion, finely chopped
1 cup / 250 ml	chopped parsley
1 tsp / 5 ml	salt
½ tsp / 2 ml	cumin
½ tsp / 2 ml	pepper
⅛ tsp / ½ ml	allspice
⅛ tsp / ½ ml	cayenne
4	hard-boiled eggs, shelled
1 cup / 250 ml	tomato sauce
½ cup / 125 ml	water

Place all ingredients, except eggs, tomato sauce and water, in a food processor, and process into a thick paste. Divide into 4 balls, then flatten out into 4 rounds. Place an egg in the middle of each round, then form into a ball with meat covering the entire egg. Place in a casserole, then pour in tomato sauce and water. Place in a 300° F (150° C) preheated oven, then cover and bake for 1½ hours or until meat is cooked.

Remove from oven and allow to cool for 15 minutes, then slice balls into ½-inch (13-mm) thick slices. Place on serving platter, then spread casserole sauce over top and serve warm.

Kufta Nayya —BISON TARTARE

Serves about 8 as an appetizer

This dish originated in the mountain villages of Lebanon, where raw meat dishes are a delicacy. Strangely, only in a few other areas of the Greater Syria region are raw meat dishes on the menu. This dish, similar to the Australian tartare, makes a great gourmet appetizer and a conversation piece for those who are trying it for the first time. The meat should be tender, preferably from a young bison.

1 lb / 454 g	bison tenderloin, cut into small pieces
1 cup / 250 ml	chopped parsley leaves
4 Tbsp / 60 ml	chopped fresh mint leaves
4 Tbsp / 60 ml	chopped coriander leaves
1 tsp / 5 ml	salt
½ tsp / 2 ml	pepper
¼ tsp / 1 ml	allspice
1	small Spanish onion, very finely chopped
2	green onions, finely chopped
2 Tbsp / 30 ml	olive oil

Place all ingredients except onion, green onions and oil in a food processor and process into a smooth paste. Transfer to a mixing bowl and thoroughly mix with the Spanish onion. Spread evenly on a platter, cover with plastic wrap, then chill in a refrigerator for 2 hours. Sprinkle with green onions and the olive oil and serve with crusty bread, fresh mint leaves, pickles and olive oil.

Kubba Nayya —FRESH BISON-BURGHUL TARTARE

Serves 6 to 8 as an entree and 12 as an appetizer

I n the land of its origin, *kubba* is made from the freshest of lamb, along with *burghul*, onions and spices. Known as *kubba* in classical Arabic, as *kibba* in the Syrian dialect, as *kibbeh* in Lebanon, as *kibbe* among the Arab immigrants in Brazil and as *kipe* on some of the Caribbean Islands, this mouth-watering dish is everyone's favourite. It is the national dish of Syria and Lebanon and, in its various forms, is one of the favoured foods among the Jordanians, Palestinians, Iraqis and other peoples in the Middle East. Those who have been nourished in their formative years on *kubba* carry their love for this dish to wherever they settle.

In the traditional method for preparing *kubba*, the meat was first pounded using a stone mortar and wooden pestle; any intact muscles were removed, then the *burghul* and the other ingredients were added and these were all pounded together. It was a messy, labour-intensive effort that took an hour or more to complete, but it produced delicious *kubba*. Today, modern implements such as grinders and food processors are used.

Anyone who has a taste for French or Australian tartare will enjoy this related dish that can be served as an appetizer or even as an entree.

Kubba Nayya should always be eaten immediately after preparation.

1 cup / 250 ml	fine *burghul*
1½ lbs / 680 g	fresh bison tenderloin, cut into pieces
2	medium onions, finely chopped
1½ tsps / 7 ml	salt
1 tsp / 5 ml	crushed dried mint leaves
¾ tsp / 3 ml	pepper
¾ tsp / 3 ml	cumin
½ tsp / 2 ml	allspice
¼ tsp / 1 ml	cinnamon
⅛ tsp / ½ ml	cayenne
	a few sprigs of fresh mint
2 Tbsp / 30 ml	olive oil

Soak *burghul* for 15 minutes in warm water, then drain by pressing water out through a fine strainer. Set aside.

Place bison tenderloin in a food processor and process until well ground, then add remaining ingredients, except *burghul*, sprigs of mint and olive oil, and process into thick paste. Transfer to mixing bowl, add the *burghul*, then thoroughly knead. Spread on a platter, then decorate with mint sprigs. Sprinkle with olive oil just before serving.

NOTE: *As a youth, I enjoyed eating this dish by scooping the* kubba *with round, pliable loaves of Arab bread, freshly cooked by my mother. We would tear a piece of this bread, then fold it in the form of a tiny shovel to scoop the Kubba Nayya into our mouths.*

kubba stuffing

Instead of being served raw, *kubba* can be stuffed and cooked in various ways.

½ lb / 227 g	bison tenderloin, ground or cut into very small pieces
3 Tbsp / 45 ml	butter
¼ cup / 60 ml	pine nuts or chopped walnuts
1	medium onion, finely chopped
½ tsp / 2 ml	salt
¼ tsp / 1 ml	nutmeg
¼ tsp / 1 ml	allspice
¼ tsp / 1 ml	black pepper

If bison is not ground, cut into ¼-inch (6-mm) cubes.

In a frying pan, melt butter, then sauté meat until it begins to brown. Stir in remaining ingredients, then sauté further until onion is limp. Set aside for use as stuffing.

kubba bil saneeya —KUBBA PIE

Serves 6 to 8

Beginning in the last half of the twentieth century, especially among the immigrants in the Western world, grinders replaced the messy hand-pounded method used for untold centuries to make *kubba*. Later, these were replaced by food processors, and the preparation of *kubba* became an even simpler matter. Despite these modern technological advancements in *kubba*-making, its labour-intensive history means that this dish is still associated with much work, and thus its preparation is usually reserved for weekend dinners, festivals and holidays.

For a busy homemaker, this type of cooked *kubba* is the easiest to make. Only a few moments are needed to ready the *kubba* for cooking. The *kubba* squares can be served either as appetizers or as a main course.

one *Kubba Nayya* recipe (see page 15)

one Stuffing recipe (see page 16)

butter or ¼ cup / 60 ml oil

Divide *kubba* into two portions. Spread one portion on the bottom of a greased 9 x 13 inch (23 cm x 33 cm) baking pan. Spread stuffing evenly over top, then flatten remaining portion of the *Kubba Nayya* over the stuffing. Cut into 2 x 2 inch (5 cm x 5 cm) diamond or square shapes, then dot with butter or spread ¼ cup (60 ml) oil over the top.

Bake for 1¼ hours or until well cooked in a 300º F (150° C) preheated oven, then remove and serve.

kubba fried —STUFFED AND FRIED

Serves 6 to 8

When I was growing up in southern Saskatchewan, I remember the countless times my mother made us the various types of *kubbas* and how each time we found that we enjoyed our *kubba* dishes more than the time before. Not only to us but to the immigrants from the Greater Syria area spread throughout the world, *kubba* evokes memories of their land of origin. Traditions, language and the Arab way of life all may be forgotten, but not the various types of *kubbas*.

This dish is usually made into egg-shaped spheres. In fact, the word *kubba*, which comes from the Arabic verb meaning "to form into a ball," has taken its name from this form. My prediction is that these balls will soon be competing with other foods in the fast-food outlets of North America as they now do in Brazil. This dish can also be made without stuffing: form the *Kubba Nayya* into balls the size of large walnuts, then deep-fry; serve as appetizers.

one *Kubba Nayya* recipe (see page 15)

one Stuffing recipe (see page 16)

oil for frying

Place in the palm of one hand a ball of *Kubba Nayya* (about the size of a golf ball). Using a forefinger, press a hole and begin expanding the hole by rotating and pressing against your palm until you have a shell of ¼ inch (6 mm) thickness. Place a heaping tablespoon of stuffing into the hollow shell. Close end of shell, then form into an egg-like shape. (Use cold water on hands to help shape and close shells.)

Deep-fry *kubba* in oil over medium heat, turning until golden brown. Serve hot.

ĸabab bil ᶜasal —HONEY KEBABS

Serves 4 to 6 as an entree

"Thy lips, Oh my spouse, drop as the honeycomb; honey and milk are under thy tongue." So celebrates the biblical "Song of Solomon" in praise of honey. To the ancients, this natural confection had a reputation as an aphrodisiac, but, above all, it was nature's foremost elixir, renowned for its culinary uses and as a cure for the many ailments of humankind. The first sweetener known to man and the only food that does not spoil, honey has been a favourite food of humans since the dawn of history. For untold centuries throughout the world, it has been utilized as a tasty stamina booster and as a cure-all medicine. A genuine and very sweet syrup, honey is rich in many vital minerals and is an easily assimilated source of energy, an instant strength-building food.

Today these delicious honey-sweet types of kebabs are found in southern Spain, no doubt introduced by the Arabs.

2 lbs / 907 g	bison tenderloin steak	Cut bison steak into 1½- to 2-inch (4- to 5-cm) cubes.
5 Tbsp / 75 ml	honey	
¼ cup / 60 ml	olive oil	Thoroughly mix all ingredients except meat, then add meat cubes and stir until they are coated with seasoning mix. Let stand for about four hours, stirring occasionally to re-coat the cubes.
1½ tsps / 7 ml	salt	
1 tsp / 5 ml	garlic powder	
1 tsp / 5 ml	paprika	
½ tsp / 2 ml	cumin	Place on skewers and grill over a low flame, basting with the remaining seasoning juice, until meat turns brown. Remove from skewers and serve as appetizers or serve hot off the skewers as an entree.
½ tsp / 2 ml	black pepper	
⅛ tsp / ½ ml	cayenne	
4 Tbsp / 60 ml	finely chopped coriander leaves	

Kufta —MEATBALLS

Serves 4 as an entree

These meatballs had their origin in the eastern Arab world and were brought by the Arabs to Spain, where they are still made today. Somehow, over the centuries they lost their Arabic name. The Spanish today call them by another Arabic name—*albóndigas*—a name derived from the Arabic *al-bunduq* (the hazelnut).

The balls are usually served as appetizers but can be served as an entree with cooked rice or mashed potatoes.

1 lb / 454 g	finely ground bison
1	medium onion, finely chopped
1	small hot pepper, finely chopped
2 Tbsp / 30 ml	finely chopped coriander leaves
2	eggs, beaten
½ cup / 125 ml	fine bread crumbs
1 tsp / 5 ml	oregano
½ tsp / 2 ml	pepper
¼ tsp / 1 ml	allspice
1½ tsps / 7 ml	salt, divided
	oil for frying
4	cloves garlic, crushed
2 Tbsp / 30 ml	flour
¼ cup / 60 ml	red grape juice
1½ cups / 375 ml	water

In a mixing bowl, place ground bison, onion, hot pepper, coriander, eggs, bread crumbs, oregano, pepper, allspice and 1 tsp (5 ml) of the salt, then thoroughly mix. Form into smaller than walnut-size balls and set aside.

In a saucepan, pour oil to about ¾ inch (2 cm) depth, then heat. Fry meatballs over medium-low heat until they turn golden brown, turning them over once. Remove with a slotted spoon, then set aside.

Discard oil with the exception of 2 Tbsp (30 ml). Add remaining ½ tsp (2 ml) of salt, garlic and flour, then stir-fry over medium heat until flour turns light brown. Add meatballs, grape juice and water, then thoroughly mix and bring to a boil. Cover and cook over medium-low heat for 10 minutes, stirring a few times and adding a little water if necessary. Serve hot.

saneeyat laham wa burghul
—MEAT AND BURGHUL PIZZA

Makes two 12-inch (30-cm) diameter pizzas

Pizzas can be made with just a few ingredients or with many. In their most primitive form, they are prepared from thin dough covered with tomatoes, cheese and a few herbs or spices, then baked. One or the other of three herbs—basil, marjoram and oregano, known as the "three pizza spices"—is utilized. However, cooks often substitute others according to taste.

As to toppings and dough, the possibilities are endless. Besides tomatoes and cheese—usually mozzarella or Parmesan—countless other foods can be used as toppings. Anchovies, clams, mushrooms, olives, onions, peppers, shrimp and various types of sausages can all be employed to enrich basic pizzas. For the dough, ground meat, potatoes, chickpeas, *burghul* and other dried products may be substituted for flour. By varying the ingredients, versatile cooks can easily serve a "new" pizza creation each time they decide to offer this gourmet delight.

1 cup / 250 ml	fine burghul
2 lbs / 907 g	ground bison round steak
1	large onion, finely chopped
4	cloves garlic, crushed
4 Tbsp / 60 ml	olive oil
1½ tsps / 7 ml	salt
2 tsps / 10 ml	dried basil, divided
1 tsp / 5 ml	pepper
½ tsp / 2 ml	allspice
¼ tsp / 1 ml	cayenne
4	medium tomatoes, thinly sliced
½ cup / 125 ml	grated Parmesan cheese

Soak *burghul* in warm water for 10 minutes, then press all water out through a sieve.

Thoroughly combine the *burghul* with the ground bison, onion, garlic, olive oil, salt, 1 tsp (5 ml) of the basil, pepper, allspice and cayenne. Spread on two greased 12-inch pizza pans, to about ½ inch (13 mm) in thickness. Cover evenly with the tomato slices, then sprinkle with the cheese and the remaining 1 tsp (5 ml) dried basil.

Bake in a 300° F (150° C) preheated oven for 1¼ hours or until edges brown. Cut into thin wedges, then serve as appetizers.

sfeehah bi khubz ᶜArabi —PITA BREAD PIZZA

Serves up to 12

Inf a Roman legionnaire from the time of Julius Caesar entered a North American pizzeria, no doubt he would think that the pizzas offered today are merely a highly exaggerated version of one of his home-cooked dishes. Made of unleavened dough, sprinkled with a few herbs and, at times, covered with onions, these ancient, simple Roman pies are the direct ancestors of our pizzas.

And although many pizzas today are far richer than their Roman predecessors, some types have changed very little in the intervening centuries. For instance, the aroma-diffusing thyme pies sold in food stalls throughout the Middle East are closely related to the Roman pizzas. They are a reminder that the products of our pizzerias have been with us for over 2,000 years.

3	loaves pita (Arab) bread, each 8 inches (20 cm) in diameter
1	large sweet pepper, finely chopped
1	large onion, finely chopped
4	cloves garlic, crushed
½ lb / 227 g	fried bison sausages, cut into very small pieces
1 tsp / 5 ml	oregano
1 tsp / 5 ml	salt
1 tsp / 5 ml	pepper
3	large tomatoes, thinly sliced
½ lb / 227 g	grated mozzarella cheese
4 Tbsp / 60 ml	olive oil

Pull pita bread apart to make 6 circles and place on greased pans. Combine sweet pepper, onion, garlic, bison sausage, oregano, salt and pepper, then spread evenly on bread. Top with tomatoes, then sprinkle with cheese and olive oil.

Bake in a 300° F (150° C) preheated oven for 30 minutes or until edges of bread turn dark brown. Cut circles into pieces and serve as appetizers.

Fatayer Laham wa Labana —MEAT-YOGURT PIES

Makes 30 small 3-inch pies; 18 medium 4-inch pies; or 12 large 6-inch pies

These pies can be made very small, medium size, or large enough for a one-person meal. The petite and medium versions can be served as appetizers, for snacks, as part of buffet meals or as supplements to soups and salads. King-size and baked, they make a delectable and filling all-in-one entree. Also excellent for lunches and as picnic fare, they add much to the culinary world of sandwich-type foods.

In the Middle East, there are various types of meat pies, usually made with lamb or beef. For me, this bison/yogurt pie stands at the top of the list.

1½ lbs / 680 g	frozen bread dough, thawed (or use homemade)
1 lb / 454 g	bison round steak, cut into tiny pieces
2 cups / 500 ml	*labana** or cream cheese
1	large onion, finely chopped
1 tsp / 5 ml	salt
¾ tsp / 3 ml	pepper
½ tsp / 2 ml	cinnamon
½ tsp / 2 ml	ground coriander seeds
⅛ tsp / ½ ml	cayenne

Thaw the dough if frozen, then cut into 12 equal pieces.‡ Roll into balls, then cover and allow to rest for one hour.

Fry bison steak pieces over medium-low heat for 15 minutes.

Prepare a filling by thoroughly combining the fried steak pieces with the remaining ingredients.

With a rolling pin, roll each ball of bread dough to a 6-inch (15-cm) round. Divide filling into 12 equal portions, then place one portion on each round. Bring edges of dough together to form a triangle and close firmly by pinching the edges.

Place the pies in a well-greased baking pan, then bake in a 300° F (150° C) preheated oven for 1 hour or until pies turn golden brown. (If a darker colour is desired, brown lightly under the broiler.)

Brush the tops of pies with butter or oil, then serve hot.

.

* Labana can be purchased in many Middle Eastern stores. TO MAKE YOUR OWN: for 2 cups of labana, place 8 cups of yogurt in a cheesecloth bag, then tie with a string and suspend over a receptacle. Allow to drain for 48 hours.

‡ For appetizers, divide and roll dough into approximately 30 3-inch rounds or 18 4-inch rounds. Divide filling accordingly, and bake as for the large pies.

Mazzat Batata wa Laham
—POTATO-MEATBALL APPETIZER

Makes about 3 dozen small balls

Potatoes, called the "noblest of vegetables," are one of the healthiest foods in the human larder. An easily grown plant, potatoes have the ability to provide more nutritious food faster on less land than any other food crop and in almost any habitat. They are jam-packed with fibre, minerals—chiefly potassium—protein, vitamins A, C and D, and complex carbohydrates, the body's main source of fuel. A 6-ounce potato has about 120 calories, is virtually fat-free and contains no cholesterol and only a small amount of sodium. Potatoes provide more protein and calories than any other food crop—five times more than corn, soybeans or wheat.

The Incas, who first grew the potato, cherished its medicinal qualities. They believed that potatoes made childbirth easier and used them to treat all types of injuries. Over centuries of seafaring, potatoes were a staple aboard ship, as the large amount of vitamin C that potatoes contain (most of which is lost if cooked for over 15 minutes) made them ideal for preventing scurvy. Also, potatoes can help in weight-loss diets since they quickly make one feel full.

1 lb / 454 g	ground bison
3 cups / 750 ml	mashed potatoes
2 cups / 500 ml	finely chopped green onions
1 cup / 250 ml	finely ground bread crumbs
4 Tbsp / 60 ml	tomato paste
2	cloves garlic, crushed
1 tsp / 5 ml	salt
1 tsp / 5 ml	pepper
1 tsp / 5 ml	ground coriander seeds
½ tsp / 2 ml	ground fennel seed
¼ tsp / 1 ml	cayenne
2 Tbsp / 30 ml	olive oil

Thoroughly combine all ingredients, then form into walnut-sized balls, adding a little water if too stiff or a little flour if too soft, and set aside.

Place balls in a greased pan, then bake in a 300° F (150° C) preheated oven for about 1¼ hours or until they turn brown. Place on serving platter and serve as appetizers.

Merguez —SAUSAGE

Serves about 4

This spicy North African sausage is found not only in its homeland, North Africa, but also in all the large cities of France, in demand by the North African community there and by a good number of French nationals as well. *Merguez* is made with lamb and/or beef and is heavily spiced; made with bison meat, it is even better-tasting. The paprika used gives the sausage a red colour. In North Africa, this tasty sausage is usually grilled and served with couscous. It is also often an ingredient in pizzas, soups and stews and is succulent when served for breakfast with fried eggs, as a lunchtime snack or as an appetizer.

In the recipe below, bread crumbs have been added so that the *merguez* can be made into patties. However, if cleaned intestines are to be used as casings, the bread crumbs can be omitted.

1 lb / 454 g	ground bison
1	medium onion, chopped
6	cloves garlic, crushed
2 Tbsp / 30 ml	finely chopped fresh coriander leaves
3 Tbsp / 45 ml	olive oil
1 tsp / 5 ml	paprika
1 tsp / 5 ml	salt
½ tsp / 2 ml	ground fennel seeds
½ tsp / 2 ml	ground coriander seeds
½ tsp / 2 ml	ground caraway seeds
½ tsp / 2 ml	ground cumin
½ tsp / 2 ml	pepper
¼ tsp / 1 ml	cinnamon
¼ tsp / 1 ml	cayenne
2 Tbsp / 30 ml	finely ground bread crumbs
	cooking oil

Place all ingredients, except cooking oil, in a food processor, then process into a smooth paste. Form into patties and set aside.

In a frying pan, place cooking oil to about ½ inch (13 mm) depth and heat, then fry patties over medium heat until they turn brown, turning them over once. Drain on paper towels, then serve hot with salad and fried potatoes.

sujuk —SAUSAGE ROLLS

Makes 20 to 30 pieces, depending on length

Usually made with paper-thin bread, this very tasty dish found in Aleppo makes a great appetizer. The culinary art of Syria's second-largest city took shape over centuries, as culture after culture flowed through this ancient trading centre. Legend has it that the prophet Abraham paused in Aleppo to milk his cows on the spot on which the city's Citadel now stands—hence, its Arabic name *Halab*, which means "milk." Located at the crossroads of great and historic commercial routes, Aleppo was for hundreds of years the terminus of the famous Silk Road. Its history is documented from the misty days of early civilizations until our times. Hittites, Akkadians, Assyrians, Eblans, Egyptians, Armenians, Persians, Greeks, Romans, Byzantines and Arabs all left traces of their foods. *Sujuk* is likely of Armenian origin.

1 lb / 454 g	ground bison tenderloin
4	cloves garlic, crushed
1 tsp / 5 ml	salt
1 tsp / 5 ml	paprika
½ tsp / 2 ml	ground coriander
½ tsp / 2 ml	cumin
½ tsp / 2 ml	ginger
½ tsp / 2 ml	turmeric
½ tsp / 2 ml	allspice
¼ tsp / 1 ml	nutmeg
¼ tsp / 1 ml	cayenne
1½ lbs / 680 g	frozen bread dough, thawed (or use homemade)
4 Tbsp / 60 ml	olive oil

Place all ingredients, except bread dough and oil, in a food processor and process into a smooth paste. Set aside.

Roll bread dough into a rectangle about ⅛ inch (3 mm) thick—the thinner the better. Spread the paste over the whole surface of the dough. Roll tightly in jelly roll fashion then cut into 1- to 2-inch (2.5- to 5-cm) rounds and place on a greased cookie tray. Sprinkle with half the olive oil, then bake in a 300° F (150° C) preheated oven for about 1 hour or until the tops begin to brown. Remove from oven and brush again with remaining oil. Serve warm.

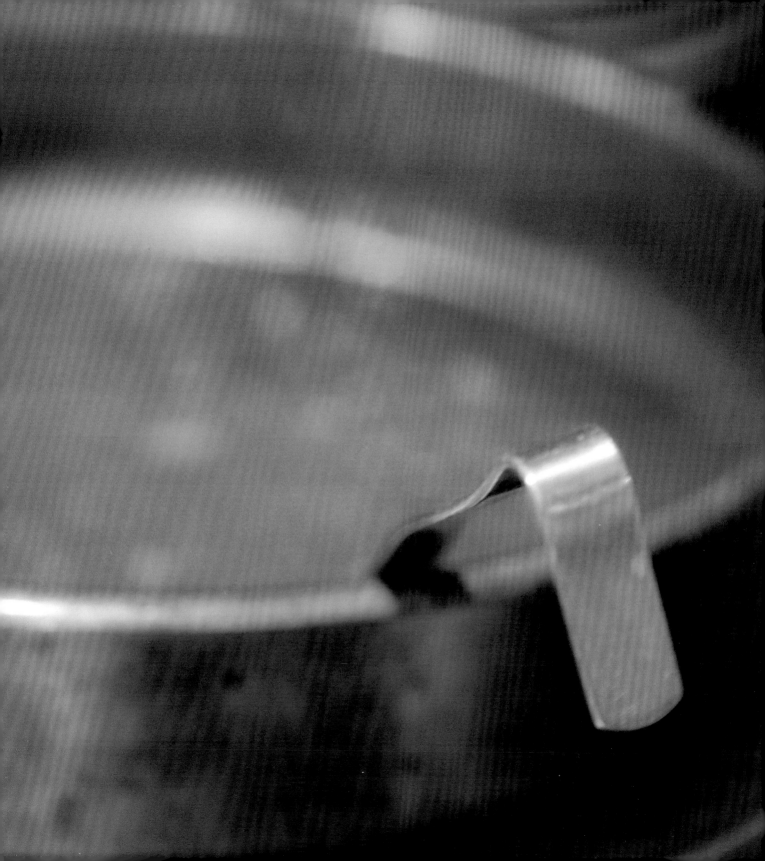

CHAPTER 3

soups

*"Soup puts the heart at ease,
calms down the violence of hunger,
eliminates the tension of the day,
and awakens and refines the appetite."*

—GEORGES AUGUSTE ESCOFFIER

Soups have been on the everyday menu of the Arab kitchen since the dawn of history. At very little cost, the farmers of the Arab world and surrounding countries enjoy healthy and nutritious broths that were developed by their ancestors. These soups, often made with whatever ingredients were at hand, have sustained generation after generation.

Many Arab emigrants, like my parents who came from Syria to western Canada in the early 1920s, brought these basic recipes with them to their new homes in North America. On our south Saskatchewan homestead, my mother prepared most of the soup recipes that I have included in this section. However, she cooked them with lamb or beef and whatever spices or herbs were available at hand. Through the Great Depression we survived and were generally healthy due to the consumption of healthy, simple dishes popular in Syria. While our neighbours found great difficulties in obtaining enough food to sustain themselves, we always had our stock of dried chickpeas, lentils and *burghul*, as well as some chickens and a few cows and sheep. Even in times of extreme hardship, such as in 1937 when a severe drought gripped southwest Saskatchewan, my parents were able to cope.

These three foods—chickpeas, lentils and *burghul*—kept us well-fed and healthy. Fresh from our hand-watered garden in summer and dried in winter, they were prepared with herbs and spices and, along with *qawarma* (recipe on page 108), became the substance of our lives.

As the basis for many types of savoury soups, they graced our table day after day. These appetizing soups were superb for all types of meals and snacks. Often we relished them as the main course, especially during the cold winter. At other times, they whetted our appetite for the meal to come. On numerous occasions, we enjoyed them as snacks, especially as a late-evening treat. On cold winter days we consumed them for breakfast and, strange as it may sound, they were excellent as a recuperative after a night of festivity.

These soups that we relished I now also prepare with bison meat, together with the soup-making staples of the Middle East—*burghul*, chickpeas, fava (broad) beans, lentils and rice. Like their Middle Eastern counterparts made with beef or lamb, these soups are wholesome, tasty and simple to prepare, and most can be served as a one-dish meal. All that is needed to complete the repast is Arab bread (pita), or bread toasted and buttered, and perhaps a salad.

Keep in mind, as well, that a number of the bison stew dishes in chapter 4 can be transformed with added water into succulent soups, fit for the tables of the elite. ❧

shawrabat fasoolya —BEAN AND MEAT SOUP

Serves 8 to 10

A good number of Middle Eastern soups are enriched by first sautéing some of the vegetables with herbs, especially fresh coriander, making them tasty as well as wholesome. These hot soups not only satisfy hunger and are healthy, but also give warmth and pleasure to the diner.

1 1/2 cups / 375 ml	navy beans
1 lb / 454 g	bison shoulder meat
4 Tbsp / 60 ml	olive oil
1	large onion, finely chopped
2 Tbsp / 30 ml	grated ginger
2	cloves garlic, crushed
1/2 cup / 125 ml	finely chopped coriander leaves
1	small hot pepper, finely chopped
8 cups / 2 L	water
2 tsps / 10 ml	salt
1 tsp / 5 ml	pepper
1 tsp / 5 ml	cumin
4 Tbsp / 60 ml	lemon juice
4 Tbsp / 60 ml	finely chopped parsley

Soak navy beans in water for 24 hours. Drain.

Cut bison meat into 1/2-inch (13-mm) cubes.

Heat oil in a saucepan, then sauté meat, onion, ginger, garlic, coriander leaves and hot pepper over medium-low heat for 10 minutes. Add beans and water and bring to a boil, then cover and cook over medium-low heat for 2 1/2 hours or until beans are well cooked, stirring a few times and adding more water if necessary. Set aside and allow to cool.

When cool, purée in a blender, then return to saucepan and bring to a boil, adding more water if necessary. Stir in remaining ingredients, except parsley. Cover and cook over medium-low heat for 5 minutes, stirring a few times. Place in bowls, then garnish with parsley before serving.

shawrabat fool wa laham
—BEAN-VEGETABLE-MEAT SOUP

Serves 8 to 10

This wholesome and hearty soup is more like a stew. It is great in winter as the main meal of the day, giving warmth and a feeling of contentment to the body. I can still remember my mother's words as she served us dishes such as this one: "You will stay strong and healthy if you always eat soups and stews."

½ lb / 227 g	bison shoulder meat
1	medium potato
4 Tbsp / 60 ml	olive oil
2	medium onions, finely chopped
4	cloves garlic, crushed
1	small hot pepper, finely chopped
1½ cups / 375 ml	skinned and split large dried fava or lima beans
2 cups / 500 ml	stewed tomatoes
1	medium carrot, finely chopped
½ cup / 125 ml	finely chopped coriander leaves
2 tsps / 10 ml	salt
1 tsp / 5 ml	pepper
1 tsp / 5 ml	cumin
8 cups / 2 L	water

Cut bison shoulder into ½-inch (13-mm) cubes.

Peel potato and dice into ½-inch (13-mm) cubes.

Heat oil in a saucepan, then sauté meat, onions, garlic and hot pepper over medium-low heat for 10 minutes. Add remaining ingredients and bring to a boil. Cover and cook over medium-low heat for 2½ hours or until beans and meat are well cooked, stirring a few times and adding more water if necessary.

shawrabat Laham —BISON MEAT SOUP

Serves 6

Soups are some of the most cherished of foods, nourishing the body and helping to keep away afflictions.

½ lb / 227 g	bison round steak
4	cloves garlic, crushed
5 cups / 1250 ml	water
4 Tbsp / 60 ml	butter
4 Tbsp / 60 ml	flour
2 cups / 500 ml	milk
¼ tsp / 1 ml	cayenne
2 tsps / 10 ml	salt
1 tsp / 5 ml	pepper

Cut bison steak into ½-inch (13-mm) cubes.

Place meat, garlic and water in a saucepan, then bring to a boil. Cover and cook over medium-low heat for 1½ hours or until meat is well cooked.

Melt butter in another deep saucepan, then stir-fry flour in the butter until flour begins to brown. Pour in meat and broth from the other saucepan, then stir in remaining ingredients. Stirring constantly, bring to a boil, then cook over low heat for 10 minutes. Serve piping hot.

shawrabat burghul wa bayd
—BURGHUL AND EGG SOUP

Serves about 8

Simple to prepare, the ancient food *burghul* is inexpensive, natural, wholesome and a succulent, versatile cereal. Often utilized as a replacement for rice, it is cooked in the same fashion as that grain, taking about 20 minutes to cook. Used in all types of dishes, it can be employed in every course and every meal of the day.

Burghul can be purchased in bulk or packaged. It comes in three sizes: coarse, medium and fine. Coarse *burghul* is utilized in soups, potage dishes and side dishes, medium *burghul* in salads and stuffings, and fine *burghul* as a main component in vegetarian and meat patties, as a breakfast cereal or as a principal element in some desserts.

4 Tbsp / 60 ml	cooking oil
½ lb / 227 g	ground bison
1	medium onion, finely chopped
4	cloves garlic, crushed
2 Tbsp / 30 ml	finely chopped coriander leaves
1	small hot pepper, finely chopped
½ cup / 125 ml	coarse *burghul,* rinsed
4 Tbsp / 60 ml	tomato paste, diluted in 1 cup (250 ml) water
2 tsps / 10 ml	salt
½ tsp / 2 ml	pepper
½ tsp / 2 ml	allspice
7 cups / 1750 ml	water
2	eggs, beaten
4 Tbsp / 60 ml	lemon juice
2 Tbsp / 30 ml	finely chopped fresh mint

In a saucepan, heat oil, then sauté ground bison over medium-low heat for 5 minutes. Add onion, garlic, coriander leaves and hot pepper, then sauté for a further 10 minutes, stirring often. Stir in the *burghul* and stir-fry for another 2 minutes, then add the diluted tomato paste, salt, pepper, allspice and water and bring to a boil. Cover and cook over medium-low heat for 1 hour, then stir in eggs, lemon juice and mint. Serve immediately.

shawrabat malfoof —CABBAGE SOUP

Serves about 10

A member of the cruciferous family that includes Brussels sprouts, broccoli, cauliflower, collards, kale and kohlrabi, cabbage is one of the most ancient of vegetables. It has been on the tables of mankind, especially those of the working class, for untold centuries. One of the most nutritious vegetables cultivated by man, it is packed with vitamins and minerals. Taking only three months' growing time, it yields large harvests and stores well. The acreage of cabbage yields more edible vegetables than the acreage of any other plant consumed. Hence, for thousands of years it was a God-sent food to peasants.

The original homeland of cabbage was likely China, where it is still extensively cultivated. In that land, it has been credited for saving millions during times of famine. The cabbage travelled to Europe at some time in history, perhaps some 2,500 years ago. Due to its storage qualities and resistance to cold, it became a major crop on the continent. In the mid-sixteenth century, French explorer Jacques Cartier brought cabbage to the Americas where, as in Europe, it became much favoured by the working class and farmers.

For centuries, even in North America, cabbage has been an important food for the poor. Some say that the part of Toronto, Ontario, called "Cabbage Town" gets its name from the Irish immigrants who moved to the neighbourhood beginning in the mid-nineteenth century. They were so poor that they grew cabbage in their front yards as one of their main food sources. Other historians say that cabbage was so inexpensive during World War II that it was on the daily menu of the inhabitants in the area and that "Cabbage Town" got its name because of the aroma of cabbage flowing out of the kitchens in that section of the city.

½ lb / 227 g	bison round steak
1	medium carrot
1	medium potato
4 Tbsp / 60 ml	butter
1	large onion, finely chopped
4	cloves garlic, crushed
3 cups / 750 ml	shredded cabbage
½ cup / 125 ml	finely chopped fresh thyme or 2 tsps (10 ml) dried thyme
2 cups / 500 ml	stewed tomatoes
7 cups / 1750 ml	water
2 tsps / 10 ml	mustard seeds
2 tsps / 10 ml	salt
1 tsp / 5 ml	pepper
1 tsp / 5 ml	cumin
¼ tsp / 1 ml	cayenne

Cut bison steak into ½-inch (13-mm) cubes. Peel carrot and potato and dice each into ½-inch (13-mm) cubes.

Melt butter in a saucepan, then sauté meat, onion and garlic over medium-low heat for 10 minutes. Add cabbage, carrot and thyme, then stir-fry for a further 5 minutes. Add remaining ingredients, then bring to a boil. Cover and simmer over medium-low heat for 1½ hours or until meat and vegetables are well done, adding more water if necessary.

shawrabat Laham wa jazar
—CARROT AND BISON SOUP

Serves about 8

The carrot, one of the main ingredients in this soup, is known as *jazar* in Arabic today, but in the medieval world it was called *isfariniyah* by the Arabs in North Africa and Arab Spain, a name that came into Spanish as *zanahoria*, the same word used for this vegetable in the Spanish-speaking world today.

4 Tbsp / 60 ml	olive oil
1 lb / 454 g	ground bison
2	medium onions, finely chopped
1	hot pepper, finely chopped
4	cloves garlic, crushed
2 Tbsp / 30 ml	grated fresh ginger
2 cups / 500 ml	finely chopped carrots
6 cups / 1500 ml	water
1 cup / 250 ml	fresh or frozen corn
2 cups / 500 ml	tomato juice
4 Tbsp / 60 ml	finely chopped coriander leaves
2 tsps / 10 ml	salt
1 tsp / 5 ml	pepper

Heat oil in saucepan, then sauté ground bison, onions, hot pepper, garlic and fresh ginger over medium-low heat for 10 minutes. Add carrots and water, then bring to a boil and cover. Cook over medium-low heat for 50 minutes, adding more water if necessary. Stir in remaining ingredients, then cook for a further 30 minutes or until meat and vegetables are done.

shawrabat karaz wa laham
—CHERRY–BISON MEAT SOUP

Serves about 10

The cherry is one of the world's oldest cultivated fruits and is believed to have been grown first in China. It became popular in the Greek and Roman worlds and the Romans spread its cultivation throughout their empire—as far away as Britain. Their bright red colour and tart/sweet taste made cherries a choice fruit on the tables of the elite in China, Greece and Rome.

The name is derived from the Assyrian *karsu* or the Greek *kerasos,* which is the name of the Turkish town of Cerasus.

Canned cranberries instead of fresh sour cherries can be used in this recipe. If fresh cherries are used, it will be quite a task to remove the pits.

1 lb / 454 g	bison round steak
4 Tbsp / 60 ml	olive oil
1	large onion, finely chopped
½ cup / 125 ml	finely chopped coriander leaves
4	cloves garlic, crushed
2 tsps / 10 ml	salt
1 tsp / 5 ml	pepper
1 tsp / 5 ml	cumin
½ cup / 125 ml	finely chopped fresh mint
½ cup / 125 ml	lentils
¼ tsp / 1 ml	chilli powder
8 cups / 2 L	water
19 oz / 540 ml	canned pitted sour cherries with their juice (not sweetened)

Cut bison steak into ½-inch (13-mm) cubes.

Heat oil in a saucepan over medium-low heat, then sauté meat, onion, coriander leaves and garlic for 10 minutes. Add remaining ingredients except sour cherries, then bring to a boil. Cover, then cook over medium-low heat for about 1½ hours or until the lentils and meat are well cooked. Stir in sour cherries and cook for a further 5 minutes, then serve.

shawrabat нummus wa ɓatata
—CHICKPEA AND POTATO SOUP

Serves about 10

Chickpeas are commonly used across the Middle East and North Africa. In the North African countries, where they are employed extensively in cooking, many believe that chickpeas increase the energy and sexual desires of both men and women. In his book *The Perfumed Garden*, Shaykh 'Umar Abu Muhammad, a sixteenth-century North African Arab writer, suggests chickpeas as a cure for impotence and as a first-rate sexual stimulant. In the eastern Arab lands, the peasants believe that chickpeas provide the essential energy necessary for their lives of toil.

1 cup / 250 ml	dried chickpeas
8 cups / 2 L	water
½ lb / 227 g	bison round steak
4 Tbsp / 60 ml	olive oil
2	medium onions, finely chopped
4	cloves garlic, crushed
4 Tbsp / 60 ml	finely chopped coriander leaves
4	medium tomatoes, chopped
1	medium potato, peeled and chopped into small pieces
2 tsps / 10 ml	salt
1 tsp / 5 ml	cumin
1 tsp / 5 ml	pepper
1 tsp / 5 ml	ground coriander seeds
¼ tsp / 1 ml	cayenne

Wash chickpeas and soak overnight, then drain.

Place the chickpeas and water in a saucepan, and bring to a boil. Cover, then cook over medium heat for about 2 hours or until the chickpeas are tender.

In the meantime, cut bison steak into ½-inch (13-mm) cubes.

Heat the oil in a frying pan, then sauté meat and onions over medium-low heat for 10 minutes. Stir in garlic, coriander and tomatoes, then cover and cook over low heat for 10 minutes. Add the frying pan contents and remaining ingredients to the chickpeas, then bring to a boil. Cook over medium-low heat for 1¼ hours or until meat and potato are cooked, adding more water if a thinner soup is desired.

shawrabat ruzz wa hummus
—CHICKPEA AND BROWN RICE SOUP

Serves about 10

Brown rice contains calcium, iron, phosphorus, protein, potassium, sodium, and the vitamins thiamine, riboflavin and niacin. It is easily digested and aids in the assimilation of other foods. Also, it is nutritious and very palatable. When milled by hand, as is done by the farmers of Asia, brown rice is a better source of protein than wheat.

Almost free of cellulose, brown rice leaves very little residue in the intestines. For diabetics, it is a good source of carbohydrates because very little insulin is needed to assimilate its starches. For hundreds of years, the vitamin B_1 (thiamine) in brown rice protected the peasants of Asia from the dreaded disease beriberi.

The only drawback of brown rice is that it takes longer to cook. Because it is easily infected with weevils, great care is needed in its storage.

If brown rice is not available, white rice can be substituted. The taste will not vary much, but the health benefits will be lost.

½ lb / 227 g	bison round steak	Cut bison steak into ½-inch (13-mm) cubes.
5½ oz / 156 ml	tomato paste	Dilute tomato paste in ½ cup (125 ml) water. Set aside.
4 Tbsp / 60 ml	olive oil	Heat oil in a saucepan, then sauté meat, onions, garlic and hot pepper over medium-low heat for 10 minutes, stirring often. Add remaining ingredients, except coriander leaves, then bring to a boil. Cover, then cook over medium-low heat for 1½ hours or until the meat is cooked. Stir in coriander leaves, then serve.
2	medium onions, finely chopped	
4	cloves garlic, crushed	
1	small hot pepper, finely chopped	
19 oz / 540 ml	chickpeas, canned, with the water	
1 tsp / 5 ml	salt	
1 tsp / 5 ml	thyme	
1 tsp / 5 ml	pepper	
1 tsp / 5 ml	cumin	
8 cups / 2 L	water	
½ cup / 125 ml	brown rice, rinsed	
4 Tbsp / 60 ml	finely chopped coriander leaves	

shawrabat Hindba wa ᶜAdas
—DANDELION-LENTIL SOUP

Serves 10 to 12

The botanical name for the dandelion—*taraxacum*—means "remedy for disorders," an indication that dandelions have been employed as a medicine for many centuries. In traditional Chinese medicine, the dandelion was considered a powerful liver tonic, relieving liver conditions such as hepatitis, gallstones and jaundice. During the Middle Ages, Arab physicians prescribed dandelion as a tonic for eye disorders and stomach ailments. European medieval herbalists also made fantastic claims about the medicinal qualities of dandelions. Some employed them to improve eyesight and in the treatment of dandruff, itching, pimples and numerous related afflictions, while others claimed that they helped relieve urinary and similar disorders.

Modern medicine has scientifically proven that most of the medieval prescriptions were not figments of the imagination. A healthful and appetizing food, dandelions are rich in minerals and nutrients. They have an abundance of vitamins A and C, calcium, iron and potassium, as well as small amounts of carbohydrates, fibre, magnesium, protein and fat. They contain as much iron as spinach and 3 times more than other similar vegetables; 50 times more vitamin A than asparagus, 25 times more than tomato juice and 7 times more than lettuce or carrots.

When my mother prepared this soup during our homesteading years, often the dandelion was replaced by other available greens such as spinach or Swiss chard.

½ lb / 227 g	bison round steak
4 Tbsp / 60 ml	cooking oil
1	large onion, finely chopped
4	cloves garlic, crushed
1	small hot pepper, finely chopped
1 Tbsp / 15 ml	grated fresh ginger
1 cup / 250 ml	lentils, rinsed
9 cups / 2250 ml	water
1 lb / 454 g	dandelions, thoroughly washed and chopped
2 tsps / 10 ml	salt
1 tsp / 5 ml	cumin
1 tsp / 5 ml	pepper
4 Tbsp / 60 ml	lemon juice

Cut bison steak into ½-inch (13-mm) cubes.

Heat oil in a saucepan, then sauté meat, onion, garlic, hot pepper and ginger over medium-low heat for 10 minutes. Add lentils and water and bring to a boil, then cover and cook over low heat for 1¼ hours. Stir in remaining ingredients except lemon juice, then bring to a boil. Cover and cook over low heat for 20 minutes, then stir in lemon juice. Serve hot.

shawrabat fool harr —HOT FAVA BEAN SOUP

Serves 8 to 10

fava beans, or broad beans, were known in the classical Hellenic world, but were not much appreciated. The Greeks believed that fava beans made them dull and caused them to have horrible dreams. On the other hand, in the Egypt of the Pharaohs, both rich and poor loved the taste of fava beans, and since that time this vegetable has graced the tables of the inhabitants of the Nile Valley. The peoples of the Indian subcontinent have enjoyed the culinary delights of fava beans for thousands of years. Today, rare is the garden in India or Pakistan that does not have at least one patch of this historical vegetable. The cool climate of Europe is ideal for the growing of fava beans, and from Roman times to the discovery of the Americas, fava beans were the only edible beans known to the inhabitants of that continent. In pre-Columbus Europe, this legume, which some have labelled the "bean of history," nourished all strata of society. It was only after the discovery of the New World that newly introduced beans from the Americas replaced the Old World fava bean.

In this recipe, you can substitute split dried lima beans for the fava beans.

4 Tbsp / 60 ml	olive oil
1 lb / 454 g	ground bison
2	medium onions, finely chopped
1	large sweet pepper, finely chopped
1	large hot pepper, finely chopped
4	cloves garlic, crushed
4 Tbsp / 60 ml	finely chopped coriander leaves
2 cups / 500 ml	stewed tomatoes
1 cup / 250 ml	split dried fava beans (or split dried lima beans)
½ cup / 125 ml	lentils, rinsed
2 tsps / 10 ml	salt
1 tsp / 5 ml	cumin
1 tsp / 5 ml	thyme
1 tsp / 5 ml	pepper
½ tsp / 2 ml	ground caraway seeds
7 cups / 1750 ml	water

Heat oil in a saucepan, then sauté ground bison, onions, sweet pepper, hot pepper, garlic and coriander over medium-low heat for 10 minutes. Stir in remaining ingredients and bring to a boil, then cover and cook over medium-low heat for 1¼ hours, stirring a number of times and adding more water if necessary. Serve hot.

shawrabat ᶜadas —LENTIL SOUP

Serves 8 to 10

According to historians, the lentil was one of the first food plants to be brought under cultivation in the Middle East. In that part of the world, where civilization began, this legume has been a part of the diet for millennia. Only bread and rice are believed to have been on the human menu for a longer period.

Lentils have been found in ancient Egyptian tombs and, since the era of the Pharaohs, have been the main staple of the Egyptian and other Middle Eastern peasants. In the Bible, Esau sold his birthright to his twin brother Jacob for a bowl of lentils, King David received a gift of lentils from Sheba and lentils were an ingredient in Ezekiel's bread. In the Qu'ran, lentils are among the foods that the Israelites in the desert asked Moses to provide for them.

½ lb / 227 g	bison round steak
1 cup / 250 ml	lentils, rinsed
7 cups / 1750 ml	water
5 Tbsp / 75 ml	olive oil
2	medium onions, finely chopped
4	cloves garlic, crushed
½ cup / 125 ml	finely chopped coriander leaves
2	large tomatoes, finely chopped
2 tsps / 10 ml	salt
1 tsp / 5 ml	cumin
½ tsp / 2 ml	pepper
¼ tsp / 1 ml	allspice
¼ tsp / 1 ml	cayenne

Cut bison steak into ½-inch (13-mm) cubes.

Place lentils and water in a pot, then bring to a boil. Cook over medium heat for 15 minutes.

In the meantime, heat oil in a frying pan, then sauté meat over medium-low heat for 5 minutes. Stir in onions, garlic and coriander leaves, then sauté for a further 8 minutes. Add tomatoes, then sauté for a further 5 minutes.

Add frying pan contents and remaining ingredients to lentils. Cover pot and bring to a boil, then simmer over low heat for about 1½ hours, adding more water if necessary. Serve hot.

shawrabat ᶜadas —IRAQI-STYLE LENTIL SOUP

Serves 6 to 8

Lentil soup is often served during Ramadan (the Muslim month of fasting), but is popular throughout Iraq at any time of the year. This soup is somewhat different than those found in the Greater Syria area. Although most of the dishes served in the restaurants of the larger cities like Baghdad are standard Middle Eastern and international foods, Iraq does have a distinctive style of cooking, with food that is milder and less spicy than some of the neighbouring countries.

1 cup / 250 ml	dried split red lentils
8 cups / 2 L	water
4 Tbsp / 60 ml	cooking oil
1	large onion, finely chopped
½ lb / 227 g	ground bison
2	cloves garlic, crushed
2½ tsps / 12 ml	salt, divided
1½ tsps / 7 ml	pepper, divided
1 tsp / 5 ml	ground coriander seeds, divided
4 Tbsp / 60 ml	butter
1 tsp / 5 ml	ground cumin
½ tsp / 2 ml	turmeric
2 Tbsp / 30 ml	lemon juice

Place lentils and water in a saucepan and bring to a boil, then cover and cook over medium-low heat for 40 minutes or until lentils turn mushy. Set aside.

Heat oil in a frying pan, then sauté onion over medium heat until golden brown. Set aside.

In the meantime, thoroughly combine ground bison, garlic and ½ tsp (2 ml) of the salt, ½ tsp (2 ml) of the pepper and ½ tsp (2 ml) of the coriander, then form into marble-size balls.

Heat butter in a frying pan, then fry meatballs until golden brown.

Stir into the lentils, the onions, meatballs, remaining salt, pepper and coriander, as well as the cumin and turmeric, then cook over medium-low heat for a further 10 minutes, adding more water if necessary. Stir in lemon juice and serve.

shawrabat laham wa makaroona
—PASTA AND BISON MEAT SOUP

Serves 8 to 10

As is common to the countries hugging the Mediterranean, Libyan cuisine has been influenced by a series of other kitchens, especially those of the Italians and of other Arabs. The pasta dishes, such as this one, can be traced to the Italian colonialists who once controlled the most fertile parts of the country.

1 lb / 454 g	bison round steak
4 Tbsp / 60 ml	tomato paste
4 Tbsp / 60 ml	olive oil
1	large onion, finely chopped
4	cloves garlic, crushed
1	small hot pepper, finely chopped
1 Tbsp / 15 ml	grated fresh ginger
2 tsps / 10 ml	salt
1 tsp / 5 ml	dry mint
1 tsp / 5 ml	cumin
1 tsp / 5 ml	ground coriander seeds
½ tsp / 2 ml	pepper
7 cups / 1750 ml	water
1 cup / 250 ml	small pasta
2 Tbsp / 30 ml	lemon juice

Cut bison steak into ½-inch (13-mm) cubes.

Dilute tomato paste in 1 cup (250 ml) water. Set aside.

Heat oil in a saucepan, then sauté meat over medium-low heat for 5 minutes. Add onion, garlic, hot pepper and ginger, then sauté over medium-low heat for a further 10 minutes, stirring often. Add the remaining ingredients, except the pasta and lemon juice, and bring to a boil. Cover and cook over medium-low heat for 1 hour, stirring occasionally. Stir in pasta and bring to a boil, then cook over medium-low heat for a further 20 minutes, adding water if a thinner soup is desired. Stir in lemon juice. Serve hot.

shawrabat mash bil-tamar hindi
—TAMARIND-MUNG BEAN SOUP

Serves about 10

Besides being on the daily menu on the Indian subcontinent and southeast Asia, tamarind is used to a great extent in the Arabian Gulf countries. Mung beans, which are native to India, are used more extensively throughout the whole of Asia and in the whole of the Middle East. They are very nourishing and easy to digest, and, unlike other beans, cause hardly any gas. Mung beans are a good source of dietary fibre and also contain copper, folate, iron, magnesium, phosphorus, potassium, protein and thiamine.

They are generally used dried and whole, but at times skinned. They are often eaten as bean sprouts. At other times, the starch of the mung beans is extracted from the ground beans to make such products as jellies and noodles.

Today, mung beans are widely grown in China and India; as well, they are cultivated in the State of Oklahoma and in Australia.

2 Tbsp / 30 ml	tamarind paste
4 Tbsp / 60 ml	olive oil
½ lb / 227 g	ground bison
2	medium onions, finely chopped
1	small hot pepper, finely chopped
4	cloves garlic, crushed
1 Tbsp / 15 ml	grated fresh ginger
2 cups / 500 ml	stewed tomatoes
1 cup / 250 ml	mung beans, rinsed
2 Tbsp / 30 ml	finely chopped coriander leaves
2 tsps / 10 ml	salt
1 tsp / 5 ml	cumin
1 tsp / 5 ml	pepper
1 tsp / 5 ml	turmeric
4 Tbsp / 60 ml	chopped fresh mint

Dissolve tamarind paste in 7 cups (1750 ml) hot water. Set aside.

Heat oil in a saucepan, then sauté ground bison, onions, hot pepper, garlic and fresh ginger over medium-low heat for 10 minutes. Stir in the dissolved paste and water and the remaining ingredients, except mint, then bring to a boil. Cover and cook over low heat for 1½ hours or until mung beans are well cooked, adding more water for a thinner soup. Stir in mint and serve.

Hareera —MOROCCAN SOUP

Serves 10 to 12

In Morocco, *hareera* is served not only as a daily soup, but also to begin a feast or to break the fast in the evenings of Ramadan, the Muslim holy month. Known as the queen of Moroccan soups, it is made from available vegetables and meats and spiced to taste. A very nourishing soup, for the Moroccan poor it is, at times, the only meal of the day. This is one of the top soups in the world—refreshing, wholesome and, above all, delicious.

1 lb / 454 g	bison round steak
4 Tbsp / 60 ml	butter
2	medium onions, finely chopped
4	cloves garlic, crushed
½ cup / 125 ml	finely chopped coriander leaves
19 oz / 540 ml	canned chickpeas
2 cups / 500 ml	stewed tomatoes
½ cup / 125 ml	lentils, rinsed
9 cups / 2250 ml	water
2 tsps / 10 ml	salt
1½ tsps / 7 ml	ground ginger
1 tsp / 5 ml	paprika
1 tsp / 5 ml	pepper
½ tsp / 2 ml	cumin
¼ tsp / 1 ml	cayenne
¼ cup / 60 ml	rice
4 Tbsp / 60 ml	lemon juice

Cut bison steak into ½-inch (13-mm) cubes.

In a large saucepan, melt butter, then sauté meat over medium-low heat for 5 minutes. Add the onions, garlic and coriander leaves, then stir-fry for a further 10 minutes. Stir in the remaining ingredients, except the rice and lemon juice, then bring to a boil. Cover and cook over medium-low heat for 1 hour. Stir in rice and bring to a boil, then cook over medium-low heat for a further 20 minutes. Stir in lemon juice and serve immediately.

NOTE: *For an exotic taste, serve with an accompanying plate of dates.*

shawrabat shiʿreeya —VERMICELLI SOUP

Serves about 8

I n all Arab soups, other meats, vegetables, herbs and spices can be substituted. To do so is simply to continue and contribute to the long tradition of culinary experimentation and creation.

1 lb / 454 g	bison round steak
8 cups / 2 L	water
2 cups / 500 ml	stewed tomatoes
2 tsps / 10 ml	salt
1	medium hot pepper, finely chopped
1 tsp / 5 ml	pepper
1 tsp / 5 ml	ground cardamom seeds
1 tsp / 5 ml	cumin
1 tsp / 5 ml	oregano
1 cup / 250 ml	vermicelli, broken into small pieces

Cut bison steak into ½-inch (13-mm) cubes.

Place meat and water in a saucepan and bring to a boil. Cover and cook over medium-low heat for 30 minutes. Add the remaining ingredients, except vermicelli, then re-cover and cook over medium-low heat for 1¼ hours or until meat is well cooked. Stir in vermicelli, then cook for a further 15 minutes. Serve hot.

shawrabat bamya —OKRA-BISON SOUP

Serves 8 to 10

Okra, also known as "gumbo" and "ladies' fingers" and in Arabic as *bamya*, is often employed for flavouring and as a food thickener. Its subtle, but distinctive, eggplant-like flavour makes it an excellent ingredient in soups. The special gumminess of this vegetable produces an ideal thick and rich broth. Hence, okra is commercially grown for manufacturers who make it into a powder for thickening soups.

1 lb / 454 g	bison meat, any cut
4 Tbsp / 60 ml	butter
2	medium onions, finely chopped
4	cloves garlic, crushed
1	small hot pepper, finely chopped
2 cups / 500 ml	stewed tomatoes
6 cups / 1500 ml	water
2 tsps / 10 ml	salt
1 tsp / 5 ml	cumin
1 tsp / 5 ml	ground ginger
½ tsp / 2 ml	pepper
10 oz / 300 g	frozen okra, cut into small pieces
2 Tbsp / 30 ml	finely chopped coriander leaves

Cut bison meat into ½-inch (13-mm) cubes.

Melt butter in a saucepan, then sauté meat, onions, garlic and hot pepper for 10 minutes. Add remaining ingredients, except coriander leaves, then bring to a boil. Cover, then cook over medium-low heat for 1½ hours or until meat is well cooked, adding more water if necessary. Stir in coriander leaves, then serve hot.

shorba —YEMENI-STYLE FENUGREEK BISON SOUP

Serves 8 to 10

 fenugreek, the most prominent spice in this recipe, is a Yemeni spice *par excellence.* The most commonly used of the spices in that country, fenugreek is the base of an everyday paste-sauce called *hulbah.* It goes well with *zhug,* a similar food enhancer. These can be found in every Yemeni meal and are added to almost every non-sweet dish.

1 lb / 454 g	bison round steak
2	medium potatoes
4 Tbsp / 60 ml	olive oil
2	medium onions, finely chopped
4	cloves garlic, crushed
1	small hot pepper, finely chopped
2 tsps / 10 ml	ground fenugreek seeds
8 cups / 2 L	water
2	medium carrots, chopped into small pieces
1 cup / 250 ml	fresh or frozen green peas
2 tsps / 10 ml	salt
1 tsp / 5 ml	pepper
1 tsp / 5 ml	cumin
4 Tbsp / 60 ml	finely chopped coriander leaves

Cut bison steak into ½-inch (13-mm) cubes.

Peel potatoes and dice into 1-inch (2.5-cm) cubes.

Heat oil in a saucepan and sauté meat, onions, garlic, hot pepper and fenugreek over medium-low heat for 10 minutes. Add water and bring to a boil. Cover and cook over medium heat for 30 minutes. Add remaining ingredients, except coriander, and bring to a boil. Cook for a further 1¼ hours over medium-low heat or until both vegetables and meat are well cooked, adding more water if necessary. Stir in coriander leaves and serve.

shawrabat ʀuzz wa Laban —YOGURT-RICE SOUP

Serves about 10

The ancient Assyrians appreciated yogurt so much that they called it *lebeny*, meaning "life." The venerable yogis of India mixed yogurt with honey and called it "the food of the gods." Cleopatra bathed in this milk product to give herself a clear and tender complexion, and Genghis Khan fed it to his soldiers to give them courage. One of man's earliest prepared foods, yogurt has few equals in the folklore of the culinary arts.

Yet, although yogurt has been a cherished food in the Middle Eastern and Central Asian lands since the dawn of civilization, in the West, it was hardly known before the turn of the twentieth century. Only recently has yogurt gained universal popularity and become a staple in the diet of many North Americans. Today, its image as a life-extender has taken hold. Some label it "the miracle milk product"; others consider it "a mystery food"; romantics call it "the elixir of life."

When I was growing up on the fields of southwest Saskatchewan, far from the lands of the Middle East and Central Asia, a bowl of homemade yogurt was one of the standards of our kitchen. We would eat it to cool off from the hot summer winds, enjoy it cooked in soups and use it as a magical medicine for stomach viruses.

There is nothing more pleasing to the palate than relishing this soup served piping hot on a cold winter day.

½ lb / 227 g	bison round steak
2 Tbsp / 30 ml	olive oil
1	large onion, finely chopped
4	cloves garlic, crushed
4 Tbsp / 60 ml	finely chopped coriander leaves
7 cups / 1750 ml	water
½ cup / 125 ml	rice
1 tsp / 5 ml	salt
½ tsp / 2 ml	pepper
2 cups / 500 ml	plain yogurt
1 tsp / 5 ml	cornstarch
2	eggs, beaten
1½ tsps / 7 ml	crushed dry mint

Cut bison steak into ½-inch (13-mm) cubes.

Heat oil in a saucepan, then sauté meat over medium-low heat for 5 minutes. Add onion, garlic and coriander leaves, then sauté for a further 10 minutes. Stir in remaining ingredients except yogurt, cornstarch, eggs and mint, then bring to a boil and cover. Cook for 1¼ hours over medium-low heat. Combine yogurt and cornstarch and stir into meat mixture, then turn heat to low. Simmer for 15 minutes, stirring clockwise a number of times. Stir in eggs and mint, then serve immediately.

CHAPTER 4

stews

I was always hungry when I returned home after a long day of helping my father work in the fields. As I opened the front door, almost always the smell from the kitchen would overwhelm my senses. The aroma came streaming out of a simmering pot atop our wood and coal stove.

In summer, it was chicken or rabbit stew with fresh vegetables from the garden; in winter, the goulashes were beef or mutton with dried beans, chickpeas or lentils. During the cold winter days, after finishing our barn chores, I always looked forward to the delectable stew that my mother had prepared. The cold would fade into memory as my body warmed up, supping on that piping-hot peoples' food.

In the ensuing years, when I roamed the Middle East and North Africa, I discovered that the stews of our farming days were only a small part of the world of Arab goulashes, known in the Arab East as *yakhnis* and in North Africa as *tajines*. As I travelled from Morocco to the Arabian Gulf, I came to know a whole series of new stew dishes, a good number of which are now included in my repertoire of foods. Yet, despite my many travels, to this day what I remember most are the recipes my mother prepared for us and their appeal after a hard day's work. Intoxicating in their flavour and fragrant with their tantalizing aromas, these stews would always satisfy my hunger pangs.

To eat succulent *yakhnis* and *tajines* is a delightful experience that will likely surprise those who have never tasted these stews. Sautéing the meats with onions and garlic, then adding the other well-proportioned ingredients, produces flavours and aromas that reflect the richness of ancient civilizations. Simmering in herbs and spices, the meats and simple vegetables are transformed to create a taste that is smooth and stimulating. Like my mother's stews, these melt-in-your-mouth *yakhnis* have a delicate texture and tastiness that most Western stews fail to produce.

In Arab *yakhnis* and *tajines*, all types of inexpensive cuts of meat and fresh or dried vegetables can be utilized interchangeably. In my view, bison meat makes an outstanding replacement for any of the traditional meats used in the Middle East and North Africa. The recipes that follow—a good number of which my mother prepared (with other meats, of course) during our homesteading days in southern Saskatchewan—reflect the glory of Arab stews, with a Western twist. ❧

Al-qidra Bilawz —ALMOND BISON STEW

Serves 4 to 6

Eating Arabian goulashes is a delightful experience that will surprise those who have never tasted these delectable stews. The meats and simple vegetables are transformed to create a taste that is smooth and intoxicating. Sautéing the meats with the onions and garlic, then adding the other ingredients in ideal proportions—this produces a harmony of flavours and aromas reflecting the richness of very old civilizations. Like my mother's stews, these melt-in-the-mouth *yakhnis* and *tajines* prepared with meat and all types of vegetables, simmering in spices and herbs, generate a delicate texture and taste that most Western stews fail to produce.

This North African dish is usually made with lamb as the main ingredient, but bison makes a fine, succulent replacement.

2 lbs / 907 g	bison tenderloin
5 Tbsp / 75 ml	butter
4	medium onions, finely chopped
4	cloves garlic, crushed
2 tsps / 10 ml	salt
1 tsp / 5 ml	pepper
½ tsp / 2 ml	ground ginger
½ tsp / 2 ml	cinnamon
⅛ tsp / ½ ml	powdered saffron, dissolved in 1 Tbsp / 15 ml of water
½ cup / 125 ml	slivered almonds
4 cups / 1 L	water
½ cup / 125 ml	finely chopped coriander leaves
½ cup / 125 ml	finely chopped parsley

Cut bison tenderloin into 1-inch (2.5-cm) cubes.

Melt butter in a saucepan, then add meat, onions, garlic, salt, pepper, ginger, cinnamon and saffron, then fry for 10 minutes over medium-low heat, stirring often. Add almonds and water, then cover and cook over medium-low heat for 50 minutes or until meat is almost done, adding more water if necessary. Stir in coriander leaves and parsley, then simmer over low heat for another 15 minutes. Serve with cooked rice or couscous.

ɤakhnat fasoolya —BEAN-BISON STEW

Serves about 8

While finishing my barn chores on cold winter days, I often looked forward to the delectable stews my mother had prepared. As I supped on that piping-hot food, the cold would fade into memory and my body would warm up, nourished by the same food that has long sustained the masses, worldwide.

1 cup / 250 ml	white navy beans
7 cups / 1750 ml	water
1 lb / 454 g	bison round steak
4 Tbsp / 60 ml	olive oil
2	medium onions, finely chopped
4	cloves garlic, crushed
1	medium carrot, peeled and sliced into thin rounds
1	medium potato, peeled and chopped into medium pieces
2 cups / 500 ml	stewed tomatoes
4 Tbsp / 60 ml	finely chopped coriander leaves
2 tsps / 10 ml	salt
1 tsp / 5 ml	cumin
1 tsp / 5 ml	pepper
½ tsp / 2 ml	ground coriander seeds
¼ tsp / 1 ml	cayenne

Soak white navy beans overnight in water, enough to cover, with ½ tsp (2 ml) baking soda, then drain.

Place beans and the 7 cups (1750 ml) of water in a saucepan, then cook over medium-low heat for 1½ hours or until beans are tender. Set aside with their water.

In the meantime, cut bison steak into ½-inch (13-mm) cubes.

Heat oil in a saucepan, then sauté meat over medium-low heat for 5 minutes. Add onions and garlic, then sauté for a further 10 minutes. Stir in remaining ingredients, including the beans with their water, then cover and simmer over medium-low heat for 1½ hours or until the meat and vegetables are tender, adding more water if necessary. Serve hot with cooked rice or mashed potatoes.

markat ommalah —BISON-CHICKPEA STEW

Serves about 8

While roaming the beautiful villages of Djerba, Tunisia's paradise isle, or strolling through the ancient streets of the holy city of Kairouan, one is always tantalized by the scent of spices diffusing from exotic dishes. These enticing aromas draw travellers to sample the array of unfamiliar foods. The age-old heritage of Tunisian cooking is best exemplified, however, when the food is prepared with loving care at home. Homemade succulent dishes spiced with caraway, cinnamon, cumin, coriander, hot peppers, thyme and saffron and, artistically arranged, are pleasing to both eye and taste.

1 lb / 454 g	bison round steak	Cut bison steak into ½-inch (13-mm) cubes.
4 Tbsp / 60 ml	olive oil	Heat oil in a saucepan, then sauté meat over medium-low heat for 5 minutes. Add onions, garlic, coriander leaves and hot pepper, then stir-fry for a further 8 minutes. Stir in chickpeas, tomatoes, salt, pepper, cumin, thyme and water, then bring to a boil. Cover, simmer over low heat for 1½ hours or until meat is well cooked, adding a little more water if necessary. Stir in olives and lemon juice, then simmer over low heat for 5 minutes. Serve hot with cooked rice or couscous.
2	medium onions, finely chopped	
4	cloves garlic, crushed	
½ cup / 125 ml	finely chopped coriander leaves	
1	hot pepper, finely chopped	
2	cans of chickpeas (each 19 oz / 540 ml), with their water	
4	medium tomatoes, chopped into small pieces	
1 tsp / 5 ml	salt	
½ tsp / 2 ml	pepper	
½ tsp / 2 ml	cumin	
½ tsp / 2 ml	thyme	
3 cups / 750 ml	water	
¼ cup / 60 ml	green olives, pitted and chopped	
2 Tbsp / 30 ml	lemon juice	

Laham wa Hummus Hilu
—BISON–CHICKPEA SWEET STEW

Serves 6 to 8

Chickpeas are commonly utilized in stews in the cuisine of the Arab East. This versatile pulse can be used with all types of meats and/or vegetables. Growing up on our Saskatchewan farm, my mother made sure that a good number of the dishes that she prepared included chickpeas. In those days, none of our neighbours had heard of chickpeas. Today, Saskatchewan is the leading producer of chickpeas in Canada.

1 lb / 454 g	ground bison steak
½ cup / 125 ml	fine bread crumbs
4	medium onions, finely chopped
2	cloves garlic, crushed
1 tsp / 5 ml	salt
½ tsp / 2 ml	cumin
½ tsp / 2 ml	allspice
½ tsp / 2 ml	pepper
4 Tbsp / 60 ml	olive oil
2 Tbsp / 30 ml	maple syrup or similar syrup
2 Tbsp / 30 ml	lemon juice
2 cups / 500 ml	water
19 oz / 540 ml	chickpeas, canned, with their water

Place ground bison, bread crumbs, half the onions, garlic, salt, cumin, allspice and pepper in a food processor, then process into a paste. Form into balls the size of small walnuts, then set aside.

Heat olive oil in a frying pan, then fry meatballs on medium-low heat until they begin to brown. Remove with slotted spoon and place in a saucepan.

In the same oil (adding more if necessary), sauté remainder of onions. Transfer frying pan contents to the saucepan with meatballs. Add the remaining ingredients, adding a little additional salt and pepper if desired. Bring to a boil and cover, then cook over medium-low heat for 1 hour, adding more water if needed. Serve hot with cooked rice or mashed potatoes.

Hor'i —BISON SHANK STEW

Serves 6 to 8

"I've been invited to an authentic Yemeni feast!" Excitement gripped me as I told my friend in Sana'a, Yemen's capital, that at last I was going to sample the country's cuisine at its best. A former Yemeni Consul in Detroit, a city that has one of the largest Yemeni communities in North America, had invited us for a magnificent meal his family had prepared for business colleagues and friends.

When we arrived, it seemed that we had landed in one of the stories in *One Thousand and One Arabian Nights*. The mouth-watering aromas floating around us fit well into the atmosphere as we feasted on the foods of this ancient land from whence hailed the Queen of Sheba. As is the custom in Yemen, we ate by dipping our right hands into the savoury foods.

3 lbs / 1.36 kg	bison shoulder meat with the bones, cut into thick slices
3	medium onions, quartered
8	cloves garlic, crushed
3 cups / 750 ml	stewed tomatoes
2 tsps / 10 ml	salt
1 tsp / 5 ml	ground fenugreek seeds
1 tsp / 5 ml	pepper
1/4 tsp / 1 ml	ground caraway seeds
1/4 tsp / 1 ml	ground coriander seeds
1/4 tsp / 1 ml	ground cardamom seeds
1/8 tsp / 1/2 ml	cayenne

Place sliced bison shoulder in a 4-quart saucepan and cover with cold water to about 2 inches (5 cm) above the meat. Bring to a boil, skimming a few times. Add the onions and garlic, then cover and reduce heat to low and simmer for about 3 to 4 hours until the meat is tender, stirring a number of times and adding a little water if necessary. Stir in remaining ingredients, then simmer uncovered over medium-low heat for 1 hour or until the juice is reduced into a somewhat thick sauce. Remove from heat and serve immediately with cooked rice.

shorba leebeeya — CHICKPEA AND BISON STEW

Serves 4 to 6

Libya's cuisine has been referred to as the "cookery of the desert." While not very sophisticated, it is satisfying and mostly healthy. Although some travellers find the Libyan kitchen basic and dull, others see it as simple and tasty, as this Libyan dish will testify.

1 lb / 454 g	bison round steak
4 Tbsp / 60 ml	olive oil
1	medium onion, finely chopped
4	cloves garlic, crushed
4½ cups / 1125 ml	water
⅛ tsp / ½ ml	cayenne
2 cups / 500 ml	stewed tomatoes
2 cups / 500 ml	cooked chickpeas
1 tsp / 5 ml	salt
½ Tbsp / 7 ml	turmeric
½ tsp / 2 ml	cumin
½ tsp / 2 ml	pepper
¼ tsp / 1 ml	cinnamon
½ cup / 125 ml	broken noodles

Cut bison round steak into ½-inch (13-mm) cubes.

Heat oil in a saucepan, then sauté meat over medium-low heat for 5 minutes. Stir in onion and garlic, then sauté over medium-low heat for a further 8 minutes. Add water and bring to a boil, then cover and cook over medium-low heat for 1 hour. Stir in remaining ingredients, then re-cover and cook for a further 20 minutes, adding more water if necessary. Serve hot with cooked rice or couscous.

shawrabat/rakhnat jamus —BISON SOUP/STEW

Serves 6 to 8

This dish of Iranian origin is found in parts of Iraq and some of the Arab Gulf countries. Somewhat different than most entrees, this dish comes in two parts, making a nearly complete meal. Bison makes a fine replacement for the beef or lamb that is usually used.

1 cup / 250 ml	dried chickpeas
½ cup / 125 ml	dried white beans
1 lb / 454 g	bison shoulder meat
1	large onion, finely chopped
1	small hot pepper, finely chopped
4 Tbsp / 60 ml	chopped coriander leaves
2 tsps / 10 ml	salt
1 tsp / 5 ml	turmeric
½ tsp / 2 ml	pepper
½ tsp / 2 ml	cumin
12 cups / 3 L	water
1	large tomato, chopped
1	large potato, peeled and chopped
¼ cup / 60 ml	rice
4 Tbsp / 60 ml	lemon juice
	croutons

Soak chickpeas and beans overnight in water, to 2 inches (5 cm) above the chickpeas and beans, with ¾ tsp (3 ml) baking soda.

Cut bison shoulder into ½-inch (13-mm) cubes.

Drain chickpeas and beans, then place in a saucepan along with bison meat, onion, hot pepper, coriander leaves, salt, turmeric, pepper, cumin and water. Cover and cook over medium-low heat for about 3 to 4 hours, until the chickpeas and beans are well cooked. Add tomato, potato, and rice, then cook over low heat for another hour or until all ingredients are very well cooked, stirring often and adding more water if necessary.

Strain out the solids and set aside. Return broth to heat, adding water to make six to eight servings. Stir in lemon juice, then heat and keep hot. Finely mash solids in a serving bowl, then serve as an entree.

At the same time, serve the broth in a separate bowl as a soup, with each diner adding croutons to taste.

rakhnat Laham wa Burghul

—BISON AND BURGHUL MEATBALL STEW

Serves 6 to 8

I f it is kept in a cool, dry place, *burghul* can be stored for five years or more without spoiling. For the Middle Eastern peasants, *burghul* was an essential food. It meant they would never go hungry, since every farmer made enough *burghul* to last his family for a number of years. If there was a year when the crops did not grow, there was usually *burghul* from the year before. On our homestead in Saskatchewan our family kept up this tradition. We usually made enough *burghul* to last us for two to three years.

1 cup / 250 ml	fine *burghul*
1 lb / 454 g	ground bison steak
1	large onion, very finely chopped
1/2 tsp / 2 ml	allspice
2 tsps / 10 ml	salt, divided
1 tsp / 5 ml	paprika, divided
1/2 tsp / 2 ml	pepper, divided
1/2 tsp / 2 ml	cumin, divided
1/4 tsp / 1 ml	cayenne, divided
3 Tbsp / 45 ml	butter
2	large tomatoes, finely chopped
4 cups / 1 L	water

Soak *burghul* for 10 minutes in warm water, then squeeze water out through a sieve.

Combine well *burghul,* ground bison, onion, allspice, 1 1/2 tsps (7 ml) of the salt, 1/2 tsp (2 ml) of the paprika, 1/4 tsp (1 ml) of both the pepper and cumin, and 1/8 tsp (1/2 ml) of cayenne. Shape into small meatballs (a little smaller than walnut size) and set aside.

Melt butter in a saucepan, then add tomatoes and the remaining salt, paprika, pepper, cumin and cayenne. Fry over medium-low heat for 8 minutes, then add the 4 cups (1 L) water and bring to a boil. Add meatballs, then cover and cook over medium-low heat for 1 hour or until meatballs are well done. Serve with cooked rice or mashed potatoes.

Yakhnat Hummus/ʿAdas wa Laham
—CHICKPEA–LENTIL AND BISON STEW

Serves about 10

In order to thrive, chickpeas need a semi-arid, sandy soil, making the countries of the Middle East, North Africa and parts of southern Europe ideal for their cultivation. In these lands of the earth's earliest civilizations, chickpeas have been employed in countless dishes. In Mexico and in several other Latin American countries, they have been on the daily menu since the era of the conquistadors. By contrast, over the past few centuries in North America, chickpeas were grown solely as feed for cattle and hogs. Only in recent years have chickpeas become a common food in Canada and the United States.

The dry Canadian and American prairies are, in fact, well suited for the cultivation of this hardy Mediterranean vegetable. When my parents homesteaded in southern Saskatchewan in the early part of the twentieth century, year after year they planted gardens overflowing with chickpeas. In the all-encompassing drought of the Depression years, when hardly any grains or vegetables grew and people went hungry, we thrived on our dishes of chickpeas. Few of our neighbours had even heard of chickpeas in those days, but today in the prairie West, they are grown commercially.

1½ cups / 375 ml	dried chickpeas
1 lb / 454 g	bison round steak
4 Tbsp / 60 ml	olive oil
2	medium sweet red peppers, chopped into small pieces
2	medium onions, chopped into small pieces
1	small hot pepper, finely chopped
4	cloves garlic, crushed
2 cups / 500 ml	stewed tomatoes
½ cup / 125 ml	lentils, rinsed
4 Tbsp / 60 ml	finely chopped parsley
2 tsps / 10 ml	salt
¾ tsp / 3 ml	pepper
1 tsp / 5 ml	basil

Soak chickpeas overnight in 8 cups (2 L) water with ½ tsp (2 ml) baking soda.

Place chickpeas with their water in a saucepan and bring to a boil. Cover and cook over medium heat for 1 hour or until chickpeas are somewhat tender, adding more water if necessary. Set aside.

In the meantime, cut bison round steak into ½-inch (13-mm) cubes. Heat oil in a saucepan and over medium-low heat sauté bison meat, red pepper, onions, hot pepper and garlic for 15 minutes, stirring often. Stir in remaining ingredients, including chickpeas with their water, and bring to a boil, adding a little more water if necessary. Cover, then turn heat to low. Simmer for 1 hour or until meat and chickpeas are well cooked, adding more water if necessary. Serve hot with cooked rice or cooked *burghul* or mashed potatoes.

Tajine K'dra —ARTICHOKE-BISON STEW

Serves 6 to 8

My first introduction to *tajine*, a dish that vies with couscous as Morocco's national dish, took place in the capital city of Rabat at the home of my friend Idriss. I had first met Idriss during his student days in Toronto, after he had finished his studies at Laval University in Quebec City. Before he returned to his country, he and his wife, Amina, had spent some time as our guests and had enjoyed our home-cooked meals of Canadian and Middle Eastern foods. Often, after a meal, we would discuss the attributes of the dishes we had just consumed, and more than once Idriss or Amina had commented, "You must come to Morocco as our guests! I am sure after savouring our dishes, you will never forget Moroccan food—especially our *tajines* and couscous." I took Idriss at his word and as a result of my many trips to Morocco I became a propagandist for their unforgettable *tajines*. Here is yet another *tajine* recipe, this one using bison meat.

25 oz / 700 g	artichoke hearts (3 small cans, drained)	Drain artichoke hearts, slice each head in half, then sprinkle with lemon juice to prevent discoloration. Set aside.
4 Tbsp / 60 ml	olive oil	
2½ lbs / 1 kg	bison round steak, cut in large pieces	In a large, deep saucepan, place the oil, bison steak, butter, onions, salt, pepper, cinnamon, ginger, turmeric and cumin, then sauté over medium heat for 5 minutes. Add water to about 2 inches (5 cm) above meat and bring to a boil, then cover and cook over low heat, stirring from time to time and adding more water if necessary, for about 2 hours or until meat is well cooked. Remove the meat from the saucepan with a slotted spoon and set aside.
4 Tbsp / 60 ml	butter	
2	medium onions, finely chopped	
2 tsps / 10 ml	salt	
1 tsp / 5 ml	pepper	
1 tsp / 5 ml	cinnamon	
½ tsp / 2 ml	ground ginger	
½ tsp / 2 ml	turmeric	
½ tsp / 2 ml	cumin	Add artichoke hearts and parsley to saucepan, then cook over medium heat until sauce begins to thicken. Stir in olives and cook over low heat for a further 5 minutes, then return meat to saucepan and cook until it is thoroughly heated.
	water	
½ cup / 125 ml	chopped fresh parsley	
½ cup / 125 ml	black olives, pitted and sliced	To serve, remove meat from pot with slotted spoon, then place on serving platter. Spoon artichoke/olive mixture over the meat.

Muraq —IRAQI-TYPE BISON STEW

Serves about 8

Iraqi cuisine has a long history going back some 10,000 years to the Sumerians, Akkadians, Babylonians, Assyrians and ancient Persians. These civilizations were highly advanced in all fields of knowledge, including the culinary arts. Tablets found in the ruins left by these ancient peoples show recipes prepared in the temples during religious festivals—the first cookbooks in the world.

However, it was during the medieval era, when Baghdad was the capital of a large Muslim empire, that the Iraqi kitchen reached its zenith. After the destruction of Baghdad in 1258 CE, this world-class cuisine declined; however, in the last century it has been revived through commercial and cultural interaction with the countries of the Mediterranean area and the world beyond.

2 lbs / 907 g	bison round steak
4 Tbsp / 60 ml	butter
½ cup / 125 ml	finely chopped coriander leaves
3	medium onions, finely chopped
4	cloves garlic, crushed
4	medium tomatoes, finely chopped
4 cups / 1 L	water
2 tsps / 10 ml	salt
1 tsp / 5 ml	pepper
1 tsp / 5 ml	cumin
½ tsp / 2 ml	allspice
¼ tsp / 1 ml	cayenne
2½ cups / 625 ml	fresh or frozen peas

Cut bison steak into ½-inch (13-mm) cubes.

In a saucepan, melt butter, then add meat and sauté over medium-low heat for 5 minutes. Add coriander leaves, onions and garlic, then sauté for a further 10 minutes. Stir in tomatoes, water, salt, pepper, cumin, allspice and cayenne, then bring to a boil. Cover, then turn heat to medium-low and simmer for 1 hour, adding more water if necessary. Add peas, then simmer for a further 20 minutes or until meat and peas are cooked, adding a little more water if necessary. Serve hot with cooked rice or mashed potatoes.

Tajine fas —BISON STEW WITH PRUNES AND HONEY

Serves 4 to 6

The Arabs considered the enjoyment of savoury foods one of life's great pleasures. Hence, when they introduced fruits and vegetables into Europe, they also brought their *yakhnis* and *tajines*. Today, many stews that grace the tables of Europe have their origins in the Arab East. Without doubt, the eggplant, *hummus* (chickpea) and lentil stews found in Spain and Portugal owe their origins to dishes developed in the Middle East.

This Moroccan dish was likely first cooked in Arab Spain. When the Arabs were expelled from the Iberian peninsula, many landing in North Africa, they brought their food with them. This recipe is the same as the one prepared in Morocco, but with bison meat replacing the lamb that is usually used.

2 lbs / 907 g	bison round steak
4 Tbsp / 60 ml	olive oil
1	medium onion, finely chopped
½ cup / 125 ml	finely chopped coriander leaves
2	cloves garlic, crushed
2 tsps / 10 ml	salt
½ tsp / 2 ml	ground ginger
½ tsp / 2 ml	pepper
½ tsp / 2 ml	tarragon
½ tsp / 2 ml	cinnamon
3½ cups / 875 ml	water
2 cups / 500 ml	small prunes, pitted
2 Tbsp / 30 ml	honey
1 tsp / 5 ml	orange blossom water
2 Tbsp / 30 ml	toasted sesame seeds

Cut bison steak into 1-inch (2.5-cm) cubes.

Heat oil in a saucepan, then add meat, onion, coriander leaves, garlic, salt, ginger, pepper, tarragon, cinnamon and water. Cover, then bring to a boil. Reduce heat to low, then simmer for 1½ hours or until the meat is well cooked, adding more water if necessary. Stir in prunes and honey, then simmer over low heat for 15 minutes, stirring frequently. If more sauce is desired, add more water. Stir in orange blossom water, then bring to a boil. Place on a serving dish, then sprinkle with toasted sesame seeds. Serve immediately with cooked rice or couscous.

tajine tufaaya —EGG-ALMOND BISON STEW

Serves 4 to 6

The *tajines* of North Africa differ somewhat from the *yakhnis* of the Middle East. In these exotic lands, the stews are often sweetened with honey and fruits and decorated with nuts. Also, the North Africans have adopted, more than their counterparts in the Middle East, the herbs and spices that Arab traders carried from the East through their countries to the Iberian peninsula and Sicily. In Morocco and Algeria the dishes are generally not hotly spiced. On the other hand, the stews in Tunisia and Libya are fiery with their ginger and hot peppers.

The meats traditionally used are beef or lamb, but bison is a fine replacement.

1½ lbs / 680 g	bison round steak	Cut bison steak into 1-inch (2.5-cm) cubes.
4 Tbsp / 60 ml	butter	Melt butter in a saucepan, then add the onions, salt, pepper, paprika, cayenne, saffron and bison steak. Sauté over medium-low heat for 10 minutes, stirring often, then add water, coriander leaves and honey, and bring to a boil.
2	medium onions, finely chopped	
1½ tsps / 7 ml	salt	
½ tsp / 2 ml	pepper	
½ tsp / 2 ml	paprika	
⅛ tsp / ½ ml	cayenne	Cover, then cook over medium-low heat for about 2 hours or until the meat is well cooked, adding more water if necessary. Turn off heat and set aside.
1 pinch	saffron	
4 cups / 1 L	water	
4 Tbsp / 60 ml	finely chopped coriander leaves	Heat olive oil in a frying pan, then add almonds and sauté over low heat until they turn golden brown. Remove from oil and set aside.
3 Tbsp / 45 ml	honey	
4 Tbsp / 60 ml	olive oil	Place meat with its sauce on a serving platter, then garnish with almonds. Arrange egg quarters on top and serve hot with cooked rice or couscous.
½ cup / 125 ml	slivered almonds	
4	hard-boiled eggs, shelled and quartered	

rakhnat badhinjan —EGGPLANT STEW

Serves about 8

No matter what type of Arab stew one cooks, the taste of garlic, coriander and other herbs or spices mixed with the juices of the meat and vegetables makes every morsel an exquisite delight.

2 lbs / 907 g	eggplant
2 tsps / 10 ml	salt, divided
1 lb / 454 g	bison round steak
2	medium potatoes
4 Tbsp / 60 ml	butter
2	medium onions, finely chopped
4	cloves garlic, crushed
3 cups / 750 ml	water
2 cups / 500 ml	stewed tomatoes
1 tsp / 5 ml	pepper
1 tsp / 5 ml	ground coriander seed
1 tsp / 5 ml	cumin
1 tsp / 5 ml	oregano
¼ tsp / 1 ml	cayenne

Peel eggplant and dice into 1-inch (2.5-cm) cubes. Place eggplant cubes in a strainer, then sprinkle with 1 tsp (5 ml) of the salt. Top with a weight, then allow to drain for 45 minutes. Meanwhile, cut the bison steak into ½-inch (13-mm) cubes. Peel the potatoes and dice into ½-inch (13-mm) cubes.

Melt the butter in a saucepan, then add meat cubes and sauté over medium-low heat for 5 minutes. Stir in onions and garlic, then sauté for a further 8 minutes. Add water, then bring to a boil. Cover, then cook over medium-low heat for 30 minutes. Add eggplant cubes, the remaining 1 tsp (5 ml) of salt and the remaining ingredients, then cook for a further 50 minutes or until meat and potatoes are cooked, adding more water if necessary. Serve hot with cooked rice or *burghul* or mashed potatoes.

Tajine Qamama —FRUIT-BISON STEW

Serves 8 to 10

Tajine, similar to the French *etouffé*, is the name both for a vast number of stews found on the menus of every Moroccan eating place and for the shallow and handle-less earthenware utensil with a cone-shaped lid in which they are cooked. It derives its name from the Greek *teganon* (frying pan) and is believed to date back to the time that the Greeks were in North Africa.

Fish, chicken, lamb or other meats and a wide variety of vegetables are stewed together with fruits, olives, lemons, herbs and spices. When cooked in *tajine* earthenware, they reach their epitome of flavour. The conical lid captures the steam and juices from all the ingredients simmering together for long hours over very low heat. The result is a fragrant combination of mouth-watering flavours—tart, spicy and sweet.

4 lbs / 1.8 kg	bison sirloin steak, cut into serving pieces
6	medium onions, finely chopped
8	cloves garlic, crushed
6 Tbsp / 90 ml	olive oil
1 Tbsp / 15 ml	grated fresh ginger
2½ tsps / 12 ml	salt
1 tsp / 5 ml	pepper
1 tsp / 5 ml	cinnamon
1 tsp / 5 ml	ground coriander seeds
⅛ tsp / ½ ml	powdered saffron
5 cups / 1250 ml	water
1 cup / 250 ml	raisins, rinsed
½ cup / 125 ml	chopped dried apricots
	slivered almonds for garnish (optional)

Place bison steak, onions, garlic, olive oil, ginger, salt, pepper, cinnamon, coriander, saffron and water in a saucepan, then stir and bring to a boil. Simmer over low heat for 2 hours, adding more water if necessary, then remove meat with slotted spoon and place in a casserole. Set aside.

Add raisins and apricots to the sauce in saucepan, then cook over medium heat until sauce somewhat thickens. Pour over meat, then cover and bake in a 300° F (150° C) preheated oven for 2 hours or until meat is very tender. Serve hot with cooked rice or couscous.

Garnish with slivered almonds, if desired.

fenugreek-flavoured bison stew

Serves about 6

Indigenous to the Near East, fenugreek, which gives this dish an exotic taste, was introduced by the Arabs to China, where it still carries its Arabic name. Also known as "bird's foot," "goat's horn" and "Greek hayes," it is, in our times, cultivated extensively on the periphery of the Mediterranean, in Africa, on the Indian subcontinent and, to some extent, in the temperate zones of North America. Fenugreek is grown by some for human consumption and employed by others for its medicinal qualities or as a forage crop.

4 Tbsp / 60 ml	cooking oil
1	large onion, finely chopped
6	cloves garlic, crushed
1	hot pepper, finely chopped
2 lbs / 907 g	ground bison
1 tsp / 5 ml	ground fenugreek
3 cups / 750 ml	water
4 Tbsp / 60 ml	tomato sauce
1 tsp / 5 ml	salt
1 tsp / 5 ml	oregano
½ tsp / 2 ml	pepper

Heat oil in a saucepan, then sauté onion, garlic and hot pepper over medium-low heat for 5 minutes. Add ground bison and fenugreek, then stir-fry for a further 10 minutes. Stir in remaining ingredients and bring to a boil, then cover and simmer over low heat for 1 hour, adding more water if necessary. Serve with cooked rice or mashed potatoes.

saltah —GROUND BISON STEW

Serves about 6

*S*altah is one of the main dishes in Sana'a, the capital city of Yemen, and is considered the country's national dish. It is often served to guests, who are always offered the best the host has to offer. It is said that in the remote districts of the country, a Yemeni farmer or tribesman will shoot over the heads of travellers if they pass by without stopping to sample his hospitality. A friend of mine who has worked in and travelled to Yemen for more than 20 years has this to say about Yemeni food: "Yemeni food is simple but tasty. However, what makes it so pleasing is the hospitality accompanying it when offered to strangers."

4	medium potatoes
4 Tbsp / 60 ml	cooking oil
1 lb / 454 g	ground bison
2	medium onions, finely chopped
4	cloves garlic, crushed
3	medium tomatoes, finely chopped
1½ tsps / 7 ml	salt
1 tsp / 5 ml	ground fenugreek seeds
1 tsp / 5 ml	pepper
¼ tsp / 1 ml	ground caraway seeds
¼ tsp / 1 ml	ground coriander seeds
¼ tsp / 1 ml	ground cardamom seeds
⅛ tsp / ½ ml	cayenne
5 cups / 1250 ml	beef broth
2	eggs, beaten
2 Tbsp / 30 ml	finely chopped fresh coriander leaves

Peel potatoes and dice into ½-inch (13-mm) cubes.

Heat oil in a 3-quart saucepan, then sauté ground bison, onions and garlic over medium-low heat for 10 minutes, stirring a number of times. Add potatoes, tomatoes, salt, fenugreek, pepper, caraway, coriander seed, cardamom, cayenne and broth, then bring to a boil. Cover and cook over medium-low heat for 1¼ hours or until meat and potatoes are well cooked, adding more water if necessary. Stir in eggs and coriander leaves, then cook for a further 2 minutes. Remove from heat and serve immediately.

North African-style Bison and Potato Stew

Serves 4 to 6

Garlic and onions are regarded as essential ingredients in almost all Arab stews. To maximize their function, they are sautéed to golden brown, but never allowed to burn. To these are added numerous exotic herbs and spices, many of which were first introduced into Europe by the Arabs. Some of these condiments still carry their Arabic names. Caraway is the Arabic *karawaya;* cumin is *kammun;* ginger, *zanjabil;* saffron, *za'faran;* sesame, *simsim;* sumach, *summaq;* and tarragon, *tarkhun.* With others, such as allspice, basil, cayenne, cinnamon, coriander, mint, nutmeg, oregano, paprika, sage and thyme, they subtly transform the character of the meats and vegetables in these savoury, enticing stews.

1½ lbs / 680 g	bison round steak
3	medium potatoes
4 Tbsp / 60 ml	butter
3	medium onions, finely chopped
4	cloves garlic, crushed
2 tsps / 10 ml	salt
1 tsp / 5 ml	pepper
1 tsp / 5 ml	sage
½ tsp / 2 ml	ground caraway seeds
½ tsp / 2 ml	allspice
¼ tsp / 1 ml	cayenne
3 cups / 750 ml	water
3	medium tomatoes, sliced in half
½ cup / 125 ml	finely chopped parsley
½ cup / 125 ml	toasted slivered almonds

Cut bison steak into 1-inch (2.5-cm) cubes. Peel potatoes and dice into 1-inch (2.5-cm) cubes.

Melt butter in a frying pan, then add meat, onions and garlic. Sauté over medium-low heat for 10 minutes. Stir in potatoes, salt, pepper, sage, caraway, allspice, cayenne, and water, then bring to a boil. Cover, then cook over medium-low heat for about 30 minutes.

Transfer frying pan contents into a casserole, then arrange the tomato pieces, cut side down, on top of the stew. Cover, then bake in a 300° F (150° C) preheated oven for 2 hours or until meat is well cooked.

Garnish with parsley and slivered almonds, then serve hot from the casserole with cooked rice or couscous.

ɣakhnat ᶜadas —LENTIL AND BISON STEW

Serves 8

In Arab stews, all types of inexpensive cuts of meat and fresh or dried vegetables can be utilized interchangeably. For centuries the Arab peasants have dined on these simple dishes and in the process have learned the art of blending and balancing textures and aromas.

In the same fashion, during the cold winter months, my mother often prepared a hearty dish similar to this one, usually with beef. The tomatoes were from our preserved supply and the onions, garlic and potatoes were from those kept semi-fresh in our earthen cellar. In summer, when our garden flourished, other vegetables were used.

½ lb / 227 g	bison round steak
4	medium potatoes
4 Tbsp / 60 ml	butter
2	medium onions, finely chopped
4	cloves garlic, crushed
1	small hot pepper, finely chopped
1 cup / 250 ml	lentils, rinsed
6 cups / 1500 ml	water
2 cups / 500 ml	stewed tomatoes
1½ tsps / 7 ml	salt
1 tsp / 5 ml	cumin
1 tsp / 5 ml	pepper
½ tsp / 2 ml	turmeric

Cut bison steak into ½-inch (13-mm) cubes.
Peel potatoes and dice into ¾-inch (2-cm) cubes.

Melt butter in a saucepan, then add meat, onions, garlic and hot pepper; then simmer over medium-low heat for 10 minutes, stirring often. Add remaining ingredients, including the potatoes, and bring to a boil, then cook over medium-low heat for 1¼ hours or until meat and lentils are well done, adding more water if necessary. Serve hot with cooked rice.

shtatha zrudiya —BISON AND CARROT STEW

Serves 4 to 6

To fully appreciate Arab stews, one must eat at a villager's home. In these humble dwellings, there is always a pot of stew simmering on the fire. For large families with limited incomes—like our family on the farm—goulashes are the core of the farmhouse menu. The farmers consider them the ideal food for their way of life. Renowned for their hospitality, the Arab peasants are always ready for unexpected guests. When one arrives, the housewife exercises her inventiveness by adding a little more water and perhaps a few more vegetables to her simmering pot of *yakhni* or *tajine*. It is easy to cook a little more rice or *burghul*, generally served as side dishes. With these Arabian goulashes, and rice or *burghul*, no Arab host will be embarrassed by running out of food as he urges his guests, "The more you eat, the more we know how much you love us."

1 1/2 lbs / 680 g	bison round steak
4 Tbsp / 60 ml	olive oil
1	head garlic, finely chopped
1 tsp / 5 ml	paprika
1 tsp / 5 ml	ground caraway
2 tsps / 10 ml	salt
1/2 tsp / 2 ml	pepper
1/2 cup / 125 ml	finely chopped coriander leaves
2 cups / 500 ml	thin rounds of carrots
3 1/2 cups / 875 ml	boiling water
4 Tbsp / 60 ml	tomato paste

Cut bison steak into 1/2-inch (13-mm) cubes.

In a saucepan, sauté meat in oil over medium-low heat for 10 minutes, then add garlic and stir-fry for a further 5 minutes. Add the reminder of the ingredients except tomato paste, then bring to a boil. Cover and simmer over medium-low heat for 1 1/4 hours or until meat and carrots are cooked, adding more water if necessary. Stir in tomato paste, then simmer for a further 10 minutes. Serve hot with cooked rice or couscous.

ɣakhnat shiᶜreeɣa —NOODLE BISON STEW

Serves 4 to 6

The peoples of the ancient civilizations and later their heirs, the Arabs, all had a hand in perfecting today's Middle Eastern and North African goulashes. Arab authors who wrote about food over a thousand years ago have left us written records about these historic dishes. Cookbooks written in the Abbasid era (750 to 1258 CE) praised in a rapturous manner the succulent *yakhnis* (stews) of Baghdad and the eastern Islamic world. During the same centuries, when Spain and Sicily were both Arab lands, Arab writers described in glowing terms the delicious stews in these regions.

Using bison meat adds yet another dimension to this succulent dish.

1½ lbs / 680 g	bison sirloin steak
4 Tbsp / 60 ml	butter
2	large onions, finely chopped
2	large tomatoes, chopped
4 Tbsp / 60 ml	finely chopped fresh mint
4	cloves garlic, crushed
2 tsps / 10 ml	salt
1 tsp / 5 ml	pepper
½ tsp / 2 ml	cumin
5 cups / 1250 ml	water
2 oz / 57 g	wide noodles

Cut bison sirloin into ½-inch (13-mm) cubes.

Melt butter in a saucepan, then sauté onions over medium-low heat for 10 minutes. Add remainder of ingredients except noodles, then bring to a boil. Cover, then simmer over medium-low heat for 1 hour or until meat is tender, adding more water if necessary. Stir in noodles, then simmer for a further 20 minutes, adding more water if necessary. Serve hot with cooked rice or mashed potatoes.

Rakhnat Laham —BISON STEW

Serves 4 to 6

During my travels through the Middle East and North Africa, I discovered that the stews of our farming days were but a few examples of the world's Arab goulashes. From Morocco to the Arabian Gulf, I came to know a whole series of new stew dishes; a good number of these are now included in my culinary repertoire.

Yet, I remember most my mother's recipes and their appeal after a hard day's work. Intoxicating in their flavour and fragrance, these stews would always satisfy my hunger pangs.

2 lbs / 907 g	bison sirloin steak
1 cup / 250 ml	grapefruit juice
1 Tbsp / 15 ml	orange blossom water
½ tsp / 2 ml	cumin
½ tsp / 2 ml	ground ginger
2 tsps / 10 ml	salt
½ tsp / 2 ml	pepper
¼ tsp / 1 ml	cayenne
1 cup / 250 ml	finely chopped parsley
1 tsp / 5 ml	cornstarch, mixed with a little water
2 cups / 500 ml	water
½ cup / 125 ml	raisins

Cut bison steak into 2- to 3-inch (5- to 7.5-cm) squares. Place meat pieces in a casserole.

Combine grapefruit juice, orange blossom water, cumin and ginger, then pour mixture over meat. Refrigerate for 2 hours, turning several times. Remove meat, and add the salt, pepper, cayenne and parsley to the juice in the casserole, then thoroughly mix. Return meat to the mixture, then cover and place in a 300° F (150° C) preheated oven. Bake for 1½ hours or until meat is done, then remove meat and place in a shallow serving bowl.

Stir cornstarch into the sauce in casserole, then add water and raisins. Stir, then return to oven for about 10 minutes, adding more water if too thick. Pour the thickened sauce over the meat, then serve with cooked rice or cooked *burghul* or mashed potatoes.

Yakhnat Jamus wa Batata
—POTATO BISON STEW

Serves about 6

In the cities of the Arab East, the wealthy look down upon *yakhnis* as peasant foods. Hence, in the fine restaurants or on the tables of the opulent they are rarely found. However, to the toiling masses it is another story. A working housewife makes a stew that can last the family for two to three days. These dishes will not become tasteless or stale because, in most cases, Arab stews improve when they are reheated. Thus, the woman of the house need only cook once or twice a week, yet her family and guests will dine on gourmet meals.

3 lbs / 1.36 kg	bison sirloin steak
2	large potatoes
4 Tbsp / 60 ml	butter
4	cloves garlic, crushed
3	medium onions, sliced
2 tsps / 10 ml	salt
½ tsp / 2 ml	pepper
½ tsp / 2 ml	nutmeg
½ tsp / 2 ml	cinnamon
¼ tsp / 1 ml	cayenne
2 cups / 500 ml	stewed tomatoes
3 cups / 750 ml	water

Cut bison steak into ½-inch (13-mm) cubes.

Peel potatoes and dice into ½-inch (13-mm) cubes.

Melt butter in a saucepan, then add meat, garlic and onions. Sauté over medium-low heat for 10 minutes. Stir in remaining ingredients, including the potatoes, then bring to a boil. Cover, then cook over medium-low heat for 1¼ hours or until the meat and potatoes are well cooked, adding more water if necessary. Serve hot with cooked rice or cooked *burghul*.

Yakhnat Batata wa Banadura
—POTATO AND TOMATO BISON STEW

Serves about 8

Arab stews are simple to prepare and require scant attention. Evolving over innumerable centuries in the lands of antiquity, they have been perfected by thousands of years of civilized living. Introducing bison meat as the main ingredient in some of these stews is simply another delicious development in the long evolution of these traditional foods.

1 lb / 454 g	bison round steak
5	medium potatoes
4 Tbsp / 60 ml	olive oil
3	medium onions, finely chopped
4	cloves garlic, crushed
1	small hot pepper, finely chopped
2 tsps / 10 ml	salt
1 tsp / 5 ml	pepper
1 tsp / 5 ml	dried and crumpled basil
½ tsp / 2 ml	nutmeg
5	medium tomatoes, chopped
5 cups / 1250 ml	water

Cut bison steak into 1-inch (2.5-cm) cubes.

Peel potatoes and dice into 1-inch (2.5-cm) cubes.

Heat oil in a saucepan, then stir in meat, onions, garlic and hot pepper, and sauté over medium-low heat for 10 minutes. Add remaining ingredients, except potatoes, then cover and cook over medium-low heat for 30 minutes. Add potatoes, then cook for a further 1 hour or until the meat and potatoes are well cooked, stirring occasionally and adding more water if necessary. Serve hot with cooked rice or cooked *burghul*.

ɣakhnat Bamya wa jamus —OKRA-BISON STEW

Serves 4 to 6

Once treasured as a delicacy in Moorish Spain, the okra is a small, attractively shaped vegetable originating in Ethiopia. From that ancient land, it travelled north to the Mediterranean shores and east to India. The African Arabs, who called it *uehka* (from which the name okra perhaps was derived), carried it to West Africa and the Iberian peninsula. After the Christian conquest in Spain, it fell out of favour there, but in much of Africa and the eastern Mediterranean it thrived and became a popular food.

In the seventeenth century okra came to North America along with the West African slaves brought by the French to Louisiana. In the ensuing years it was extensively cultivated in the Mississippi delta, its original American home.

1 lb / 454 g	bison round steak
4 Tbsp / 60 ml	butter
2	medium onions, finely chopped
2	cloves garlic, crushed
1	small hot pepper, finely chopped
2 cups / 500 ml	stewed tomatoes
2 cups / 500 ml	water
10 oz / 300 g	frozen okra
4 Tbsp / 60 ml	finely chopped coriander leaves or parsley
½ tsp / 2 ml	salt
½ tsp / 2 ml	ground ginger
¼ tsp / 1 ml	pepper
4 Tbsp / 60 ml	lemon juice

Cut bison steak into ½-inch (13-mm) cubes.

Melt butter in a saucepan, then sauté meat, onions, garlic and hot pepper over medium-low heat for 10 minutes. Add tomatoes and water, then bring to a boil. Cover, then cook over medium-low heat for 50 minutes. Gently stir in remaining ingredients except lemon juice, then bring to a boil, adding more water if necessary. Simmer over medium-low heat for 25 minutes, then stir in lemon juice and serve hot with mashed potatoes or cooked rice or cooked *burghul*.

Tajine M'qualli —FAVA BEAN–BISON TAJINE

Serves about 4 to 6

In the 1980s, while travelling by bus from Casablanca to Marrakesh, I had the opportunity to sample one of these traditionally cooked *tajines*. During the journey, I became friendly with my seat companion—a jeweller from Casablanca named Muhammad. When the bus stopped for lunch, as the other passengers streamed into a roadside restaurant serving French food, Muhammad took me by the hand and steered me to a nearby people's eating place where everyone was dining on *tajines*.

As I enjoyed my succulent dish, I learned that the *tajines* were prepared the previous day and allowed to simmer all night. For only a few dirhams, I had savoured a memorable meal. As I was about to pay, Muhammad pulled my hand back, "Don't think of paying! Are we not Arabs? You are my guest!" That meal, along with Muhammad's hospitality, I have never forgotten.

That day, the *tajine* was made from lamb, but bison meat makes a succulent replacement.

1 lb / 454 g	bison shoulder, cut into serving pieces
1	large onion, finely chopped
4	cloves garlic, crushed
4 Tbsp / 60 ml	finely chopped coriander leaves
1½ tsps / 7 ml	salt
1 tsp / 5 ml	ground ginger
¾ tsp / 3 ml	pepper
½ tsp / 2 ml	turmeric
5 cups / 1250 ml	water
4 Tbsp / 60 ml	olive oil
2½ cups / 625 ml	fresh or frozen fava beans
2 Tbsp / 30 ml	lemon juice
½ cup / 125 ml	black olives, pitted and halved

In a saucepan, place meat, onion, garlic, coriander leaves, salt, ginger, pepper, turmeric, water and olive oil, then bring to a boil. Cover, then cook over low heat for 3 to 4 hours or until meat is tender, adding more water if necessary. Stir in fava beans and bring to a boil, then cook over medium-low heat for a further 20 minutes or until beans are done, adding more water if necessary. Stir in lemon juice, then place in a serving bowl. Decorate with olives, then serve hot.

fenugreek-flavoured Bison and Beans

Serves 8 to 10

fenugreek has been used for centuries in the lands of the Far East, India, Yemen, Egypt and the other Middle Eastern lands. Besides using it in their cooking, the people in these lands employed fenugreek as a health restorative and aphrodisiac. Fenugreek was introduced by the Arabs into Europe a short time before the ninth century and almost immediately met with the approval of the aristocracy. It is said that Charlemagne favoured this spice and encouraged its cultivation on the imperial farms of Germany. Nonetheless, in subsequent years its use never became widespread in western lands.

2 cups / 500 ml	dried white kidney beans (or similar type)
1 lb / 454 g	bison round steak
4 Tbsp / 60 ml	olive oil
2	medium onions, finely chopped
4	cloves garlic, crushed
1	hot pepper, finely chopped
2 tsps / 10 ml	ground fenugreek
½ cup / 125 ml	finely chopped coriander leaves
8 cups / 2 L	water
2 cups / 500 ml	stewed tomatoes
2 tsps / 10 ml	salt
1 tsp / 5 ml	oregano
1 tsp / 5 ml	pepper

Soak kidney beans overnight, then drain.

Cut bison steak into ½-inch (13-mm) cubes.

Heat oil in a saucepan, then sauté bison meat for 5 minutes over medium-low heat. Add onions, garlic, hot pepper, fenugreek and coriander leaves, then stir-fry for a further 8 minutes. Add beans and water, then bring to a boil. Cover and cook over medium-low heat for 2 hours or until beans are soft, adding more water if needed. Stir in remaining ingredients and re-cover. Cook for another 30 minutes, then serve with cooked rice or cooked *burghul*.

Bizillah Ma^c Laham Jamus
—PEAS WITH BISON MEAT

Serves about 6

I was always hungry when I returned from working with my father in the fields. As I opened the front door, the aroma from a simmering pot atop our wood and coal stove would almost always overwhelm my senses. In summer, it was chicken or occasionally rabbit stew with fresh vegetables from the garden; in winter, the goulashes were beef or mutton with dried beans, chickpeas or lentils.

Although we lived in the land of the bison, none of our family or friends had ever heard of bison meat being used in cooking. This had to wait for later years, when the bison were again to emerge on the prairie—this time on ranches.

1 lb / 454 g	bison sirloin steak or ground bison
4 Tbsp / 60 ml	olive oil
1	large onion, finely chopped
4	cloves garlic, crushed
½	small hot pepper, finely chopped
3 cups / 750 ml	water
2 cups / 500 ml	cooked tomatoes
1 lb / 454 g	shelled fresh peas or frozen peas
1½ tsps / 7 ml	salt
1 tsp / 5 ml	oregano
½ tsp / 2 ml	pepper
½ tsp / 2 ml	cumin

Cut bison steak, if using, into ½-inch (13-mm) cubes.

Heat oil in a saucepan, then add the bison meat cubes (or ground meat) and sauté over medium-low heat for 5 minutes. Stir in onion, garlic and hot pepper, then sauté for a further 10 minutes, stirring a number of times. Add water, then cover and bring to a boil. Simmer over medium-low heat for 1 hour, stirring occasionally and adding more water if necessary. Stir in remaining ingredients, then cook over medium-low heat for a further 20 minutes, adding more water if necessary. Serve hot with cooked rice or mashed potatoes.

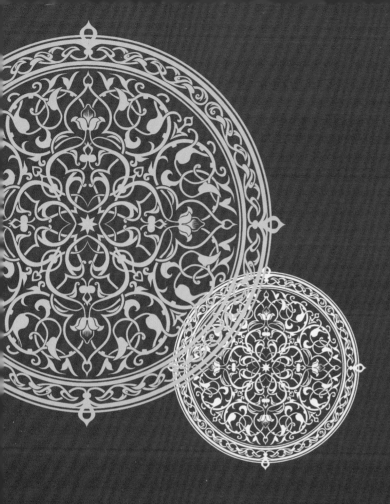

CHAPTER 5

entrees

It was not difficult for me to create recipes for bison meat entrees, since Arab cuisine is rich in meat dishes, most often using lamb or beef. If they can afford it, the Arabs in the Middle East and North Africa usually prefer meat to all other foods. This is a result of their history, the world they lived in and their environment.

Arab cuisine was born in the tents of the ancient nomads, who ate what they could carry or move with them in their desert migrations. In order to survive the harsh elements of the desert, the nomadic tribes in the Arabian peninsula relied heavily on a diet of meat— usually lamb, but also camel meat. As they moved from one grazing ground to the next, following the vegetation, most of the tribesmen would be accompanied by their flocks of sheep and, of course, their camels. Since vegetables and grains were largely unavailable in these barren lands, meat was the only staple in the desert nomad's diet.

Other foods produced by their animals— butter, milk and especially yogurt—would enhance their daily meat dishes. Complementing these animal products were dates and, when available, barley, rice and wheat. With this limited variety of ingredients, these resourceful people were nonetheless able to come up with delicious dishes that were easy to prepare, yet succulent and wholesome. Their descendants in the Arab countries have not forgotten the traditions of their forefathers. As in the past, meat remains a central part of their diet, prominent at lunch and dinner, and, at times, breakfast.

Like the Arab nomads who thrived on their limited diet, the indigenous peoples who lived on the North American plains existed for millennia almost solely on bison meat, sustained by its superior nutritive value. While they include ingredients that were not always available to these ancient wanderers, the recipes that follow nonetheless arise out of and pay homage to the rich culinary histories of both the Middle East and the Prairie West, and they promise to delight the sophisticated, modern diner even as they nourished and sustained our ancestors in both hemispheres for hundreds of generations. ❧

кufta maᶜ кaraz
—BARBECUED MEATBALLS WITH CHERRIES

Serves about 4

During my first trip to Lebanon and Syria in 1961, my love affair with *kufta* began in Aleppo. A young man with little money, I could afford to dine only in the people's eating places. Among the foods that I enjoyed during that visit was a dish I will never forget—*kufta maᶜ karaz* (barbecued meatballs with cherries). Dining at a bare wooden table set on a sawdust-covered floor, I savoured every morsel of the tasty meatballs. When I told the waiter how much I had enjoyed the *kufta*, he smiled as he quoted these words:

"Should you travel the whole world, you will never find,
Like the *kufta* of Aleppo, the best food of humankind."

The waiter was an amateur poet, as are many young men in the Arab world; however, he left such an impression on me that I have never forgotten those lines of verse.

In Aleppo, a special kind of bitter-black cherry, found only around that city, is used when preparing this dish.

1 lb / 454 g	finely ground bison
¾ tsp / 3 ml	salt
½ tsp / 2 ml	pepper
½ tsp / 2 ml	allspice
½ tsp / 2 ml	cumin
½ tsp / 2 ml	ground coriander seeds
¼ tsp / 1 ml	cinnamon
¼ tsp / 1 ml	nutmeg
⅛ tsp / ½ ml	cayenne
	cherries, large fresh pitted, or canned or candied

Place all ingredients except cherries in a food processor, then process for one minute. Form into small balls, about 1 inch (2.5 cm) in diameter, wetting hands to keep meat from sticking. Place tight on skewers, alternating meatballs and cherries. Press meatballs by hand on skewers to elongate. Barbecue until meat is done, from 5 to 10 minutes. Serve hot with cooked rice.

ʄasoolya maᶜ ᶜasal —BAKED BEANS WITH HONEY

Serves about 6

Honey was much sought-after in ancient Egypt. It was employed in lieu of gold to pay taxes, buried with the dead as sustenance for the hereafter, and offered as a food for the gods.

In the Middle East this quickest source of human vigour has been a cherished food for millennia. In Europe, before the Arabs introduced sugar, honey was virtually the only sweetener known on that continent. The Roman historian Pliny, when writing about *Arabia Felix*, indicated that the southern Arabs owed their wealth to the huge production of honey—hence, the Biblical phrase, "a land flowing with milk and honey."

1½ cups / 375 ml	white beans
1 lb / 454 g	bison round steak or ground bison
8 cups / 2 L	water
1	large onion, finely chopped
4	cloves garlic, crushed
4 Tbsp / 60 ml	tomato paste
4 Tbsp / 60 ml	honey
4 Tbsp / 60 ml	olive oil
2 tsps / 10 ml	salt
1 tsp / 5 ml	dry mustard
1 tsp / 5 ml	cumin
1 tsp / 5 ml	ground coriander seeds
½ tsp / 2 ml	pepper
¼ tsp / 1 ml	cayenne

Soak white beans overnight in water to 2 inches (5 cm) above the beans, with ½ tsp (2 ml) baking soda. Drain.

If using bison steak, cut into ½-inch (13-mm) cubes. Set aside.

Place beans and 8 cups (2 L) of water in a saucepan, then cover and cook over medium-low heat for 1 hour or until beans are half cooked (still semi-hard). Transfer with their water to a casserole, then stir in remaining ingredients, including the cubed bison steak or ground bison.

Cover, then bake in a preheated 300° F (150° C) oven for 4 to 5 hours or until both beans and meat are well cooked, checking occasionally and adding more water if necessary.

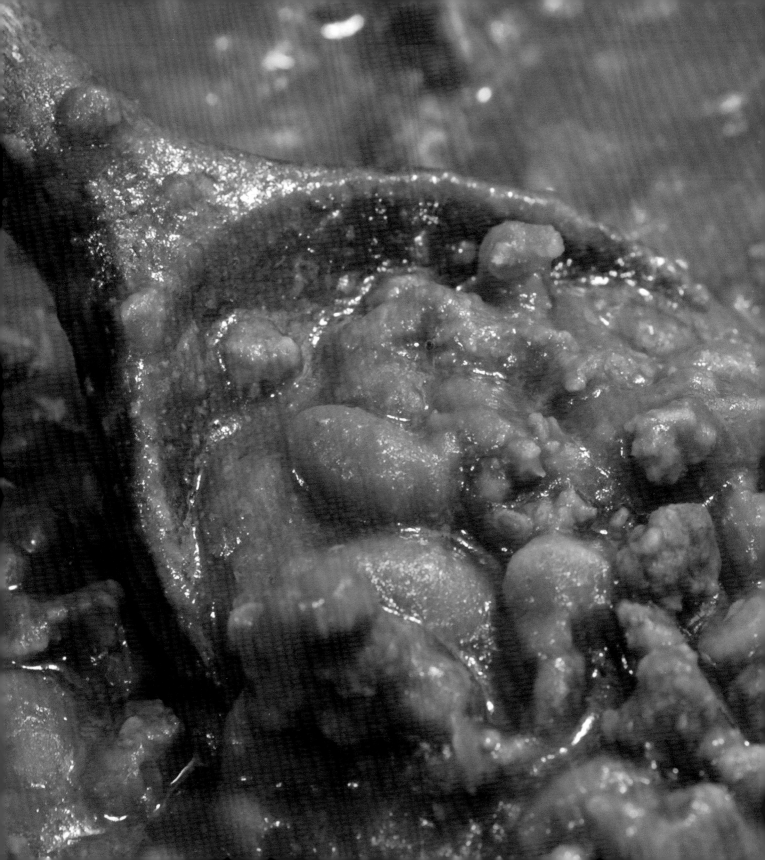

ꝺꞯwꞆꞅmꞔ —PRESERVED BISON MEAT

Makes 2 quarts (2.2 litres)

Q awarma has been eaten in the Middle East perhaps since the birth of civilization. As homesteaders in southern Saskatchewan, my parents kept up the tradition of making this type of preserved meat. All summer long, a few aged sheep or an old cow or other animals would be force-fed many times a day, and sometimes even at night, until they were loaded with fat. In the autumn, after the animals were butchered, the fat was removed and melted. The meat was then cut into very small pieces and cooked in the fat. When the meat was well cooked, it was placed along with the fat in earthenware utensils or glass jars. These were stored in a cool earthen cellar, becoming our meat supply for the following year. Since we had no refrigeration, this was an ideal way to ensure that we had meat for the whole year. During the summer months, our neighbours could only dream of roast or steak. As for our family, we always had tasty qawarma.

Qawarma scrambled eggs makes a fine breakfast dish—since the meat is already cooked, it takes only a few moments to prepare. It puts bacon and eggs to shame. This preserved meat also goes well in soups and stews, but should be added near the end of cooking, about 5 minutes before a dish is ready.

Unlike in the past, today the making of qawarma in a modern kitchen is a simple task. This recipe is a scaled-down version of our qawarma production during the years when it was the cornerstone of our daily menu.

5 lbs / 2.3 kg	bison (any cut) (mutton or beef may be substituted for bison)
2½ lbs / 1 kg	melted beef or bison fat or margarine or oil
5 tsps / 25 ml	salt
2½ tsps / 12 ml	pepper

NOTE: *Melt as much* qawarma *as needed in a recipe, then discard the fat. There is no need to refrigerate the* qawarma *if it is well cooked. If the utensils or jars are well-sealed the* qawarma *will stay usable for at least a year.*

Cut bison into ¼-inch (6-mm) cubes.

Place the melted fat or margarine or oil in a large saucepan and heat, then stir in meat, salt and pepper. Cook uncovered over medium-low heat, stirring once in a while to make sure the meat does not stick to the bottom of the pot, until the meat is well cooked (meat is well cooked when it sticks to a wooden spoon).

Allow to cool, then pour into an earthenware utensil or glass jars, making sure the meat is covered with ½ inch (13 mm) of fat. Discard the remaining fat. Store the qawarma in a cool place and always return to a cool place after use.

pemmican

Makes about 1 quart (1 litre)

Perhaps my love for *qawarma* led me to appreciate this creation of the Plains First Nations. With no refrigeration possible on the prairies during the Depression years, our family had thrived on *qawarma*, the ancient Middle Eastern method of preserving meat. In later years, I often searched for pemmican but could not find it for sale. The few times I had it in the homes of friends and acquaintances only increased my yearning for this close relative of meat jerky, South American *charqui* and South African *biltong*. Eventually, I developed my own version of this flavoured dried meat that was the mainstay of the Plains Indians and early explorers and, today, is an ideal provision for trappers and Arctic travellers.

This recipe is a simple modern method of making tasty pemmican.

2 lbs / 907 g	round bison steak
¾ cup / 175 ml	melted margarine
1 Tbsp / 15 ml	brown sugar
1 tsp / 5 ml	salt
1 tsp / 5 ml	thyme
½ tsp / 2 ml	pepper
½ tsp / 2 ml	ginger
1 cup / 250 ml	dried currants

Cut bison steak into very thin strips, then place in a greased pan. Dry in the oven, at the lowest temperature possible, until the meat turns hard. This could take up to 4 hours or more, depending on the oven temperature and on the thickness and toughness of the meat.

Place in a food processor with the remaining ingredients, then process into a paste, adding more margarine if needed. Place in a 1-quart (1-litre) plastic container with a tight lid to take along on a journey, or store container in refrigerator and serve as needed.

ragheef jamus —BISON MEAT LOAF

Serves about 8

During the Great Depression, my mother made meat loaf with all types of meats and pulses. Hers were somewhat different than the regular meat loaves known in North America, especially with respect to the inclusion of various herbs and spices. Almost every type she made was tasty, and I never tired of having them on the menu. Normally, we ate the meat loaf warm as part of the main course or as sandwiches for our school lunches.

In my re-creation of this dish I have tried to replicate my mother's meat loaf, with the added Canadian touch that bison provides.

1 cup / 250 ml	lentils
4 Tbsp / 60 ml	tomato paste
1 lb / 454 g	ground bison
4 Tbsp / 60 ml	olive oil
1	large onion, finely chopped
1	small hot pepper, finely chopped
4	cloves garlic, crushed
2	eggs, beaten
2 Tbsp / 30 ml	pomegranate syrup
1½ tsps / 7 ml	salt
½ tsp / 2 ml	mustard
½ tsp / 2 ml	pepper
½ tsp / 2 ml	cumin
½ tsp / 2 ml	rosemary
½ tsp / 2 ml	thyme
½ tsp / 2 ml	oregano
½ tsp / 2 ml	basil
½ tsp / 2 ml	sage

Soak lentils overnight, then drain.

Dissolve tomato paste in 4 Tbsp (60 ml) water.

Place lentils in a food processor and finely process, then add all the other ingredients, including the tomato paste. Process until smooth, then form into the shape of a loaf and place in a greased loaf pan. Bake uncovered in a 300° F (150° C) preheated oven for about 3 hours or until the meat loaf is well cooked. Allow to cool somewhat, then slice into ½- to 1-inch (13-mm to 2.5-cm) thick slices and serve with gravy and mashed potatoes, and ketchup or processed mustard.

Qaraas jamus wa Burghul
—BISON AND BURGHUL PATTIES

Serves about 6

This dish is another version of *kubba,* often called the king of all the foods in the Greater Syria area. In this version, vegetables are added and it becomes a somewhat different dish. It is typically made with lamb, but when prepared with bison it is even tastier, and baking the patties in the oven makes them much healthier than *kubba,* which is usually fried.

The patties can be served for snacks and appetizers or as an entree.

½ cup / 125 ml	*burghul*
1 lb / 454 g	ground bison steak
1	large onion, chopped
1	large sweet pepper, chopped
1 cup / 250 ml	mashed potatoes
2	cloves garlic, crushed
¼ cup / 60 ml	fine bread crumbs
½ cup / 125 ml	finely chopped parsley
4 Tbsp / 60 ml	finely chopped coriander leaves
2½ tsps / 12 ml	salt
1 tsp / 5 ml	pepper
1 tsp / 5 ml	cumin
1 tsp / 5 ml	ground oregano
⅛ tsp / ½ ml	cayenne

Soak *burghul* for 10 minutes in warm water, then squeeze water out through a sieve.

Place all ingredients in a blender, including the *burghul,* then blend into a bread dough consistency, adding more bread crumbs if necessary. Roll dough into walnut-size balls and flatten into patties, then place in a greased baking pan, uncovered. Bake in a 300° F (150° C) preheated oven for 1¼ hours or until done.

saneeyat Laham —BISON CASSEROLE

Serves 6

 s soon as this dish is cooked, it should be immediately removed from the oven. If left in the oven, the tomato slices will become dry. Excellent when served with fried potatoes and a tossed salad.

1 lb / 454 g	ground bison steak
1 cup / 250 ml	pulverized walnuts
2	medium onions, finely chopped
4	cloves garlic, crushed
4 Tbsp / 60 ml	finely chopped coriander leaves
1 tsp / 5 ml	crushed dried mint leaves
1 tsp / 5 ml	salt
½ tsp / 2 ml	allspice
½ tsp / 2 ml	pepper
2	medium tomatoes, sliced
2 Tbsp / 30 ml	olive oil

In a mixing bowl, thoroughly combine all ingredients except tomatoes and olive oil. Spread evenly in a greased casserole, then place tomato slices evenly over top. Sprinkle with olive oil, then cover and bake in a 300° F (150° C) preheated oven for 1½ hours or until meat is cooked. Immediately remove from oven and serve.

Laham bil furn —BISON ROAST

Serves about 6

The best and most tender bison meat comes from animals that are about 3 years old. Roasts made from tender young bison are very tasty. Meat of the older animals should be ground and made into such dishes as burgers, meatballs and meat loaf. Often only salt and pepper are used to give flavour to bison roasts, but this roast prepared Middle Eastern-style is even tastier.

3 to 4 lbs / 1.3–1.8 kg	bison rib-eye roast
8	cloves garlic, crushed
3 tsps / 15 ml	salt
1 tsp / 5 ml	pepper
1 tsp / 5 ml	cumin
1 tsp / 5 ml	ground coriander seeds
1 tsp / 5 ml	turmeric
½ tsp / 2 ml	ground cloves
½ tsp / 2 ml	chilli flakes
4 Tbsp / 60 ml	cooking oil
2 Tbsp / 30 ml	vinegar
1 cup / 250 ml	water

With a fork, punch holes into the bison roast in a number of places.

Thoroughly combine remaining ingredients, then rub over roast, forcing some of the liquid into the punched holes. Marinate in refrigerator overnight.

Place with the marinating juice in a roasting pan and cover, then roast in a 275° F (135° C) preheated oven for about 4 hours or until roast is well cooked. Baste with pan juices every 30 minutes, adding more water if the juice thickens and turning roast over once or twice. Uncover and roast at 350° F (180° C) for 20 minutes, turning over once.

Carve and serve while somewhat warm with heated pan juices and mashed potatoes.

Tamar wa Laham bil Ruzz
—BISON–DATE–RICE POTAGE

Serves 6 to 8

Dates can be eaten fresh or dried, made into jams and syrups or utilized as ingredients in the preparation of other foods, such as confectioneries, pastries and even numerous meat dishes. Dates are native to the Middle East and North Africa, where they are employed in countless dishes, from appetizers to entrees to desserts. Living in the midst of a golden harvest of dates, the peoples in these lands have long realized the value of this historic fruit.

2 lbs / 907 g	bison round steak
5 Tbsp / 75 ml	butter
2	medium onions, finely chopped
4	cloves garlic, crushed
4 Tbsp / 60 ml	finely chopped coriander leaves
2 tsps / 10 ml	salt
½ tsp / 2 ml	cinnamon
½ tsp / 2 ml	pepper
¼ tsp / 1 ml	allspice
1 cup / 250 ml	pitted dates, cut into quarters
1 cup / 250 ml	rice, rinsed

Cut bison steak into ½-inch (13-mm) cubes.

Melt butter in a saucepan, then sauté meat over medium-low heat for 10 minutes or until lightly browned. Stir in onions, garlic and coriander, then sauté further until onions begin to become limp. Add all the remaining ingredients, except dates and rice, then cover with enough water to bring the level 1 inch (2.5 cm) above the ingredients. Bring to a boil. Cover and simmer over medium-low heat for 1 hour. Stir in dates and rice, adding more water if necessary, then turn heat to low. Cover and cook for about 20 minutes or until rice is tender but not mushy, stirring occasionally to ensure that rice does not stick to bottom of saucepan, and adding more water if necessary. Serve hot.

Burghul Mufalfal maᶜ Laham
—BURGHUL POTAGE WITH BISON

Serves 4

A very versatile food, *burghul* is believed to have been first eaten in the Euphrates Valley as far back as 5,000 BCE. Since then, it has been a mainstay of Middle Eastern cuisine. In contrast, it is only in the last few decades that *burghul* has become known in Europe and North America. Introduced by Armenians, Syrians and other nationals from the Middle East, this delightful wheat product is gradually becoming known among the general public in the Western world. Easy to prepare and very delectable and nourishing, *burghul* is truly the noblest food achieved by wheat.

½ lb / 227 g	bison sirloin steak
4 Tbsp / 60 ml	butter
2	medium onions, finely chopped
2	cloves garlic, crushed
½	small hot pepper, very finely chopped
1 cup / 250 ml	coarse *burghul*, rinsed
2½ cups / 625 ml	water
¾ tsp / 3 ml	salt
¼ tsp / 1 ml	pepper
¼ tsp / 1 ml	cumin

Cut bison steak into ½-inch (13-mm) cubes.

In a frying pan, melt butter, then sauté meat over medium heat for 5 minutes. Add onions, garlic and hot pepper, then sauté over medium-low heat for a further 10 minutes, stirring often. Add *burghul*, then stir-fry for another 2 minutes. Stir in remaining ingredients and bring to a boil, then cover and cook over medium-low heat for 20 minutes, stirring a number of times, but always re-covering to make sure *burghul* does not stick to bottom of frying pan. Shut off heat and stir, then re-cover and allow to cook in its own steam for a further 30 minutes. Serve hot.

Bison shawarma

Serves 4 to 6

A delicious barbecued meat dish, *shawarma* is famous across the Middle East. In the souks and restaurants throughout the Arab East, it is not unusual to find stand-up grills of flavourful roasted meat that is thinly sliced and made into sandwiches. Nothing brings on hunger pangs more than the aroma of barbecuing *shawarma* filling the air as one passes a *shawarma* stand. This is a mini *shawarma*, but cooked in an oven.

2 lbs / 907 g	tender bison meat
4 Tbsp / 60 ml	lemon juice
4 Tbsp / 60 ml	olive oil
1 tsp / 5 ml	salt
½ tsp / 2 ml	pepper
½ tsp / 2 ml	paprika
¼ tsp / 1 ml	cumin
¼ tsp / 1 ml	ground coriander seeds
¼ tsp / 1 ml	ground ginger
⅛ tsp / ½ ml	cayenne

Cut bison meat into thin slices, about ½ inch (13 mm) wide.

Combine all ingredients, including bison meat, in a casserole and place in refrigerator overnight. Place casserole uncovered in oven and cook in a 300° F (150° C) preheated oven for 1 hour or until done but still juicy, adding a little more olive oil if needed. Serve with cooked rice or fried potatoes, or as a sandwich in (pita) bread on a bed of salad and fried potatoes.

Laham Miqlee maᶜ Habaq
—BISON STEAK WITH BASIL SAUCE
Serves 4

Pleasing to the eye, smell and taste, basil is known as the "herb of kings." In the eastern Mediterranean lands, it has long been prized above all herbs and spices. The Greeks in the ancient Hellenic era gave it the name *basileus*, a Greek word meaning "king," to indicate its position among herbs. For centuries, the nobility utilized its essence as a royal perfume and ecstatically wrote of its countless joys and, above all, its culinary benefits.

5 Tbsp / 75 ml	olive oil
2 lbs / 907 g	bison sirloin steaks
1 tsp / 5 ml	salt, divided
1 tsp / 5 ml	crushed dried thyme
½ tsp / 2 ml	pepper
⅛ tsp / ½ ml	cayenne
1	medium onion, finely chopped
4	cloves garlic, crushed
1½ Tbsp / 22 ml	flour
1 cup / 250 ml	water
2 tsps / 10 ml	dried basil

In a frying pan, heat the olive oil, then add the steaks and sprinkle with ½ tsp (2 ml) of the salt, as well as the thyme, pepper and cayenne. Sauté over medium-low heat for 8 minutes, turning steaks over a few times, then remove the rare steaks and place on a serving platter and set aside but keep warm.

If there is too much fat in frying pan, retain only 3 Tbsp (45 ml), then add onion, and sauté over medium-low heat for 10 minutes. Stir in garlic, then sauté for a further 3 minutes. Add flour, then stir-fry for 2 minutes. Stir in water and remaining ½ tsp (2 ml) of salt, then bring to a boil and simmer for about 2 minutes, stirring all the time. Stir in basil, then pour evenly over steaks. Serve immediately with mashed potatoes.

Thareed —BREAD WITH BISON AND VEGETABLES

Serves about 8

T hareed (also known as *thareedah* and *thardah*) is a dish of broken bread pieces moistened with meat or vegetable broth and was a typical Bedouin dish in pre-Islamic Arabia. Numerous recipes for *thareed* appear in tenth- to thirteenth-century Arab cookbooks, attesting to the popularity of this dish in culinary history.

2 Tbsp / 30 ml	tomato paste
4 Tbsp / 60 ml	cooking oil
1	medium onion, finely chopped
4	cloves garlic, crushed
1/2	hot pepper, finely chopped
3	medium tomatoes, finely chopped
4 Tbsp / 60 ml	finely chopped coriander leaves
2 tsps / 10 ml	salt
1 tsp / 5 ml	cumin
1 tsp / 5 ml	ground coriander seeds
1/2 tsp / 2 ml	pepper
1/4 tsp / 1 ml	ground cardamom seeds
1/4 tsp / 1 ml	caraway
1/4	lemon, finely chopped
4 cups / 1 L	water
3 lbs / 1.36 kg	bison round steak, cut into serving pieces
1/2 lb / 227 g	carrots, cut into 1/4-inch / 6-mm thick rounds
1/2 lb / 227 g	zucchini, cut into large pieces
2	medium-sized pita bread, toasted and broken into pieces

Dilute tomato paste in 1/2 cup (125 ml) water. Set aside.

Heat oil in a saucepan, then sauté onion, garlic, and hot pepper over medium-low heat for about 10 minutes. Add tomatoes, diluted tomato paste and coriander leaves, then cook over medium-low heat for 10 minutes. Stir in salt, cumin, ground coriander seeds, pepper, cardamom, caraway and lemon, then add water and bring to a boil. Add bison steak, then cover and cook for 1 hour over medium-low heat, stirring a few times and adding more water if necessary. Add carrots and zucchini, then re-cover and cook over medium-low heat for another hour, stirring often and adding more water if necessary. Arrange bread on the base of a serving bowl, then pour meat, vegetables and stock onto the bread and serve.

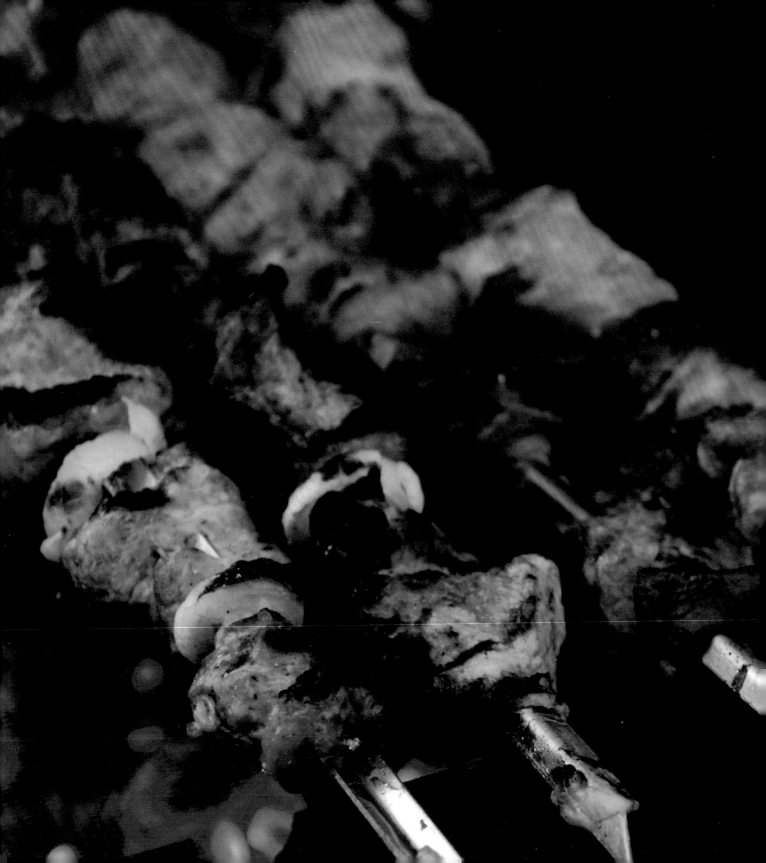

bison shish kebab

Serves 4 to 6

S hish Kebab is today a dish known all over the world, but it had its origin in the Middle East. This way of preparing shish kebab is found in the area of Iraq-Iran. Its name tells the story of the dish—*shish* is a Persian word meaning skewer and *kabab* an Arabic word meaning barbecued cubes of meat. The marinating of the meat with the onions makes it very tasty, especially when served with grilled tomatoes and rice.

2 lbs / 907 g	bison tenderloin
2	medium onions
4 Tbsp / 60 ml	olive oil
1½ tsps / 7 ml	salt
½ tsp / 2 ml	pepper
	butter
12	small tomatoes

Cut bison tenderloin into 1½-inch (4-cm) cubes.

Grate onions or process in a food processor for a minute.

Combine meat, onions, olive oil, salt and pepper, then place in refrigerator and allow to marinate for 3 to 4 hours.

Place meat on skewers, then grill, brushing occasionally with butter, until done.

Halve the tomatoes, then sprinkle with pepper and salt to taste. Place tomatoes on skewers and grill separately from the meat, then serve both together, placing meat and tomatoes over a platter of cooked rice.

sheesh вarak —DUMPLINGS IN YOGURT

Serves 8 to 10

An ancient food found in the kitchens of many lands, dumplings—in my view—reach their epitome in *Sheesh Barak,* found in the Greater Syria area. Perhaps this is because of my own experiences during my youth in western Canada. When the cold winter months rolled around, my mother often served me a steaming hot bowl of *Sheesh Barak;* the mouth-watering aroma wafting through our kitchen left me with a lasting impression.

Like numerous other non-sweet dumplings, *Sheesh Barak* served to extend small amounts of meat into gourmet meals. It was a very useful dish for the poor with large families like ours during the Depression years. Over the years, I have prepared this dish many times and every time it has had the same appeal—a wholesome and satisfying taste.

In this recipe, precautions must be taken so that the yogurt does not curdle or separate. This is done by gently stirring in one direction over low heat until it comes to a gentle boil.

DUMPLINGS

1 lb / 454 g	fresh or frozen bread dough, thawed
1 lb / 454 g	ground bison
2 Tbsp / 30 ml	butter
4 Tbsp / 60 ml	pine nuts or slivered almonds
½ tsp / 2 ml	salt
½ tsp / 2 ml	pepper
½ tsp / 2 ml	ground coriander seeds
¼ tsp / 1 ml	cinnamon
2	medium onions, finely chopped
2	cloves garlic, crushed

LABANEEYA—YOGURT SAUCE

2	eggs, beaten
3 cups / 750 ml	plain yogurt
3 cups / 750 ml	cold water
2 Tbsp / 30 ml	butter
2	cloves garlic, crushed
1 tsp / 5 ml	salt
2 Tbsp / 30 ml	dried mint

Form bread dough into 20 to 30 balls about ¾ inch (2 cm) in diameter, then cover with a tea towel and allow to rest for 1 hour.

In the meantime, to make the filling, stir-fry ground bison in butter over medium-low heat for 10 minutes, then add the remaining dumpling ingredients and stir-fry for a further 5 minutes.

Roll out dough balls to make circles ⅛ inch (3 mm) thick and about 2½ inches (6 cm) in diameter. Place 1 level teaspoon of filling on each circle, then fold dough over filling and pinch edges to seal. Fold in half again to shape dumpling like a thimble and pinch to close. Place dumplings on a greased cookie sheet and brown lightly under a broiler, turning them over once. Set aside.

To make sauce, place eggs and yogurt in a saucepan and stir until well blended. Add cold water, then stir well. Cook over medium heat and gently stir in one direction until mixture comes to a boil, then reduce heat to low.

In the meantime, melt butter in a small saucepan, then add the garlic, salt and mint. Stir-fry over medium heat until garlic turns golden brown. Stir garlic mixture into yogurt sauce. Place dumplings in sauce, then cover and cook for 30 minutes over low heat. Serve piping hot.

couscous with bison meat

Serves about 12

The first time I heard of couscous was in the 1950s when a friend of mine, a student attending the Sorbonne University, discovered this North African dish in one of the people's cafes in Paris. He became so enamoured with its mouth-watering qualities that every Sunday he would treat himself to a meal of couscous in this humble French restaurant. However, he always thought to himself that a dish so delectable and appetizing when prepared in a French eating place must be even more succulent when cooked by North Africans. On his last day in France, for an ultimate treat, he chose a classy Moroccan restaurant. It was a complete disaster. The couscous he had enjoyed for six months in the French workers' cafe was much superior in taste. My friend had discovered what many already knew: couscous had become an integral part of the French kitchen and of many other cuisines throughout the world.

1 lb / 454 g	bison sirloin steak
½ lb / 227 g	carrots
½ lb / 227 g	turnips
½ lb / 227 g	zucchini
½ lb / 227 g	pumpkin
½ lb / 227 g	cabbage
2 cups / 500 ml	couscous
4 Tbsp / 60 ml	cooking oil
3 tsps / 15 ml	salt
1½ tsps / 7 ml	pepper
1½ tsps / 7 ml	ground ginger
pinch	pure saffron
1	small bunch of parsley or coriander leaves, chopped
½ lb / 227 g	onions, chopped
¾ lb / 340 g	tomatoes, chopped
6 cups / 1500 ml	water
½ lb / 227 g	green beans or broad beans
4 Tbsp / 60 ml	butter

Cut bison steak into 1-inch (2.5-cm) cubes.

Scrape carrots and quarter them lengthwise, then cut into 2-inch (5-cm) pieces.

Peel turnips, then cut into pieces ½ inch (13 mm) thick, 1 inch (2.5 cm) wide and 2 inches (5 cm) long.

Halve unpeeled zucchini lengthwise, then cut into 2-inch (5-cm) pieces.

Peel the pumpkin, then cut into pieces ½ inch (13 mm) thick, 1 inch (2.5 cm) wide and 2 inches (5 cm) long.

Chop cabbage.

Soak couscous in warm water for a few seconds, then quickly drain and place in the top part of the couscousiére or a double boiler with a perforated top. Thoroughly break up the lumps in the couscous and set aside.

In bottom part of the couscousiére or double boiler, heat oil, then add bison meat, salt, pepper, ginger, saffron, parsley or coriander leaves, onions and tomatoes. Stir-fry for 10 minutes over medium-low heat, then add water and bring to a boil. Cook over medium-low heat for 20 minutes, then add all vegetables and bring to a boil. Fit the top part holding the couscous to the bottom part with the stew

(If steam is escaping between the two parts, seal together with a dampened, flour-impregnated piece of cloth.) Cook over medium-low heat for a further 50 minutes, stirring couscous every few minutes to make sure kernels do not stick together, then stir butter into couscous and remove from heat.

Place couscous on a platter, pyramid-style, then make a wide, deep well in the middle. With a slotted spoon, remove meat and vegetables and place in the well to fill it. The remaining meat and vegetables may be served as a side dish. Place the remaining sauce in a bowl, and serve alongside the couscous, so that each person can add sauce to taste.

muthawwim —GARLIC MEATBALLS

Serves about 10

I first became acquainted with Algerian cuisine some four decades ago, far away from its native land. An Algerian woman in Toronto introduced me to the dishes of her country. She was an excellent cook and even the dishes I later ate in Algeria could not compare to her tasty meals. Her salads and couscous dishes were unforgettable, but, above all, I remember a garlic and meatball dish called *muthawwim*, which I have often cooked since. For me, it still is the epitome of Algerian food. This recipe uses bison steak and ground bison.

1 lb / 454 g	bison round steak
4 Tbsp / 60 ml	butter
1	large onion, finely chopped
½	head garlic, peeled and crushed
1 tsp / 5 ml	salt
½ tsp / 2 ml	pepper
½ tsp / 2 ml	cinnamon
¼ tsp / 1 ml	cayenne
5 cups / 1250 ml	water
4 Tbsp / 60 ml	tomato paste
19 oz / 540 ml	can of chickpeas with its water

MEATBALLS

1 lb / 454 g	ground bison
¼ cup / 60 ml	rice, rinsed
1	small bunch parsley, finely chopped
1	egg, beaten
½	head garlic, peeled and crushed
1 tsp / 5 ml	salt
½ tsp / 2 ml	pepper
½ tsp / 2 ml	cinnamon

Cut bison steak into ½-inch (13-mm) cubes.

Melt butter in a saucepan, then sauté onion over medium heat for 10 minutes. Add cubed bison meat, garlic, salt, pepper, cinnamon and cayenne, then stir-fry for 5 minutes. Add water, then bring to a boil. Cover, then simmer over medium-low heat for 40 minutes.

In the meantime, to make the meatballs, thoroughly combine the ground bison, rice, parsley, egg and garlic, salt, pepper and cinnamon. Form into meatballs the size of a small walnut, then gently place the meatballs in the simmering saucepan.

Bring to a boil, then simmer over medium-low heat for about 10 minutes. Add tomato paste and chickpeas, then simmer over medium-low heat for 1 hour or until the meatballs are well cooked, adding more water if necessary. Serve with cooked rice or couscous.

Laham ma^c Laban —GROUND BISON WITH YOGURT

Serves 4 to 6

Cardamom gives this dish a special taste. An exotic spice sometimes called "the Seeds of Paradise," cardamom is native to India and Sri Lanka, where it is still found in the wild. Over 4,000 years ago this spice was mentioned in the sacred texts of India. There is also evidence to indicate that it was grown as an ornamental plant in the gardens of the Babylonian kings. In later centuries, adventurous Arab spice traders brought it to the ancient Egyptian, Greek and Roman worlds. For hundreds of years, it was a much-sought-after commodity, especially for use as a perfume.

Neither the Greeks nor the Romans ever knew how to obtain this spice directly from its land of origin. Using wisdom and cunning, the Arabs protected their lucrative spice trade. They deceived historians from Herodotus to Pliny into believing that cardamom was a product of Arabia when, in fact, it was imported from India.

4 Tbsp / 60 ml	cooking oil
1 lb / 454 g	ground bison
2	medium onions, finely chopped
4	cloves garlic, crushed
1 tsp / 5 ml	freshly ground cardamom seeds
½ tsp / 2 ml	ground ginger
½ tsp / 2 ml	salt
¼ tsp / 1 ml	cinnamon
⅛ tsp / ½ ml	cayenne
1½ cups / 375 ml	plain yogurt
2 Tbsp / 30 ml	finely chopped coriander leaves

Heat oil in a frying pan, then sauté ground bison over medium-low heat for 8 minutes. Stir in onions, garlic, cardamom, ginger, salt, cinnamon and cayenne, then sauté over medium-low heat for a further 15 minutes or until meat is done, stirring every few minutes and adding a little more oil if necessary. Stir in yogurt and coriander leaves, then remove from heat and serve immediately.

masbahat Darweesh — EGGPLANT-BISON CASSEROLE

Serves 8 to 10

The nutritional value of eggplant is about average, perhaps on the same level as the tomato. On the other hand, because eggplant is not high in calories, it is ideal for those who must watch their weight. Known as "the peasant's meat" in the Mediterranean countries, it is regarded as a staple. Its meaty texture makes it extremely versatile. Some have speculated that if the eggplant recipes of all the Mediterranean countries were gathered together, there would be well over a thousand. In the Arab countries of the Middle East alone, at least 150 eggplant dishes are known.

1½ lbs / 680 g	eggplant
2 tsps / 10 ml	salt, divided
1 lb / 454 g	bison round steak
2	large potatoes
2	large onions
2	medium zucchini
2	large tomatoes
½ cup / 125 ml	olive oil
4 Tbsp / 60 ml	butter
4	cloves garlic, crushed
4 Tbsp / 60 ml	finely chopped coriander leaves

1 tsp / 5 ml	pepper
1 tsp / 5 ml	cumin
½ tsp / 2 ml	cinnamon
½ tsp / 2 ml	allspice
1 cup / 250 ml	tomato juice
	water

Peel eggplant and cut into slices ½ inch (13 mm) thick. Place slices in a strainer, then sprinkle with 1 tsp (5 ml) of the salt. Top with a weight, then allow to drain for 45 minutes.

Meanwhile, prepare the other ingredients: cut the bison steak into ½-inch (13-mm) cubes; peel potatoes and onions and cut into slices ¼ inch (6 mm) thick; cut zucchini and tomatoes into slices ½ inch (13 mm) thick.

Heat oil in a frying pan, then sauté eggplant slices over medium heat for about 8 minutes or until they begin to brown, adding more oil if necessary. Remove from pan and place on paper towels to drain.

In another frying pan, melt butter, then sauté bison meat, crushed garlic and coriander leaves over medium-low heat for 10 minutes. Set aside.

In a casserole in alternating layers place the potatoes, zucchini, bison meat, eggplant, tomatoes, and lastly onions. Sprinkle over top the remaining 1 tsp (5 ml) of salt. Mix the pepper, cumin, cinnamon and allspice into the tomato juice and pour over the contents of the casserole, adding enough water barely to cover the top of the ingredients. Cover casserole, then bake in a 300° F (150° C) preheated oven for about 1½ hours or until the meat and vegetables are done. Bake uncovered for the last 10 minutes, then serve hot from the casserole.

Kufta Mabrouma —GROUND BISON WITH PINE NUTS

Serves about 6

This is a speciality of Aleppo, where it is baked and served on a round platter, with the rolls arranged in diminishing circles. Traditionally this dish is made with lamb (or sometimes beef) as the main ingredient. Tender bison meat makes a great replacement.

2	medium onions, very finely chopped
4	cloves garlic, crushed
1	egg, beaten
2 lbs / 907 g	finely ground bison tenderloin
2 tsps / 10 ml	salt
1 tsp / 5 ml	pepper
½ tsp / 2 ml	allspice
¼ tsp / 1 ml	cayenne
4 Tbsp / 60 ml	pine nuts, divided into six amounts
4 Tbsp / 60 ml	melted butter
4 Tbsp / 60 ml	water
2 Tbsp / 30 ml	coarsely chopped parsley
1	lemon, sliced

Place onions, garlic, egg, ground bison, salt, pepper, allspice and cayenne in a mixing bowl and thoroughly combine. Flatten mixture to about ¼ inch (6 mm) thickness, then cut into 6 rectangular pieces. Press pine nuts into the longer side of each piece, then roll into crescent sausage shape. Tightly fit into a round casserole, then brush with butter and sprinkle with water. Cover and bake in a 300° F (150° C) preheated oven for 1½ hours, uncovered for the last 20 minutes, or until rolls are well cooked. Place on a hot serving platter, then garnish with parsley and lemon slices. Serve with cooked rice or fried potatoes.

Kufta —GROUND BISON KEBABS

Serves 6

This Iraqi/Iranian method of preparing *kufta* puts the standard North American hamburger and all its relatives to shame.

2 lbs / 907 g	bison tenderloin steak, ground or processed until very smooth
2	medium onions, grated
2	eggs, beaten
1 Tbsp / 15 ml	lemon juice
1 tsp / 5 ml	salt
½ tsp / 2 ml	pepper
½ tsp / 2 ml	turmeric
½ tsp / 2 ml	cumin
½ tsp / 2 ml	cinnamon
½ tsp / 2 ml	thyme
	butter
12	small tomatoes, halved, then sprinkled with pepper and salt to taste

Combine all ingredients, except butter and tomatoes, mixing well until sticky. Divide into about 20 balls, then, with hands, place each ball around a skewer and mould to a cigar shape about 1½ inches (4 cm) in diameter. Grill for a few minutes on each side, brushing occasionally with butter, until done. Set aside and keep warm.

Place tomatoes on skewers and grill separately, then serve both together, placing meat and tomatoes over a platter of cooked rice.

ĸαbαb mαᶜ ĸαrαz —BISON MEATBALLS AND CHERRIES

Serves 4

O ne of the most enticing signs of spring are the beautiful blossoms of the cherry trees, which after a few months bear their tangy fruit. Besides being featured in all types of desserts, in the Syrian-Aleppo kitchen cherries are also used to give a touch of class to a wide variety of entrees.

The cherries for this dish should be sour. Canned cherries are the best, but use only those with a small amount of sugar. Do not use syrupy cherries that are meant for pies and other desserts.

1 lb / 454 g	ground bison
¼ cup / 60 ml	bread crumbs
2	eggs, beaten
½ tsp / 2 ml	allspice
½ tsp / 2 ml	ground cumin seeds
1 cup / 250 ml	very finely chopped onions, divided
1 tsp / 5 ml	salt, divided
½ tsp / 2 ml	pepper, divided
19 oz / 540 ml	canned pitted sour cherries with their juice (not sweetened)
4 Tbsp / 60 ml	tomato paste
2 cups / 500 ml	water
2 Tbsp / 30 ml	olive oil

Prepare meatballs by combining ground bison, bread crumbs, eggs, allspice, cumin and half of each of the onions, salt and pepper. Mix well and form into meatballs the size of small walnuts, then set aside.

Place the meatballs, the remaining onions, salt, and pepper, reserved cherry water, tomato paste, water and oil in a saucepan, then bring to a boil. Cover and cook over medium-low heat for about 1 hour, stirring a number of times and adding more water if necessary. Add cherries, then re-cover and simmer over low heat for about 20 minutes or until meatballs are cooked, adding more water if needed. Serve hot with cooked rice.

кabab ıroog —BISON PATTIES

Makes from 20–25 patties, depending on size

U nlike in other Middle Eastern countries, where *kababs* are usually barbecued, traditional Iraqi *kababs* are made into patties and fried. I have tried them both fried and cooked in an oven and found the oven ones preferable. To this recipe, I have added an egg, not usually included in traditional recipes for *kababs*. Typically made from either beef or lamb, these are even more succulent when made with bison meat.

1 lb / 454 g	ground bison
1	small sweet pepper, finely chopped
1	large tomato, finely chopped
1	medium onion, finely chopped
2	cloves garlic, crushed
1/2 cup / 125 ml	flour
1	egg, beaten
2 Tbsp / 30 ml	finely chopped coriander leaves
1 tsp / 5 ml	salt
1/2 tsp / 2 ml	pepper
1/2 tsp / 2 ml	cumin
1/2 tsp / 2 ml	turmeric

Place all ingredients in a food processor, then process for 1 to 2 minutes. Form into patties about 1/2 inch (13 mm) thick and place in a greased baking pan. If the mixture is too soft, spoon into the pan with a large spoon, then form into patties. Bake in a 300° F (150° C) preheated oven for 1 1/2 hours or until tops turn golden brown.

NOTE: *If these are to be fried, add more flour to stiffen the meat mixture.*

samboosa —BISON PIES

Makes 20 pies

n the Indian subcontinent, where *Samboosas* have their origins, they are usually prepared with a pastry dough and fried. This Arab/Indian version is much healthier. A spicy relative of the Arab *fatayer*, it is made with ordinary bread dough and baked in the oven.

1½ lbs / 680 g	bread dough
4 Tbsp / 60 ml	cooking oil
1 lb / 454 g	ground bison
2	medium onions, finely chopped
1	small hot pepper, very finely chopped
2	cloves garlic, crushed
4 Tbsp / 60 ml	finely chopped coriander leaves
1 cup / 250 ml	fresh or frozen green peas
2	medium tomatoes, finely chopped
1 tsp / 5 ml	ground coriander seeds
1 tsp / 5 ml	salt
1 tsp / 5 ml	cumin
½ tsp / 2 ml	pepper
¼ tsp / 1 ml	turmeric
	olive oil

Form dough into 20 balls and place on a floured tray, then cover with a lightly dampened cloth and allow to stand in a warm place for 30 minutes.

Heat oil in a frying pan and sauté ground bison over medium-low heat for 8 minutes, then add onions, hot pepper, garlic and coriander leaves. Sauté over medium-low heat for a further 5 minutes, then stir in remaining ingredients except olive oil, and sauté for a further 3 minutes. Set aside as filling.

With a rolling pin, flatten balls into 5- to 6-inch (12- to 15-cm) rounds, then set aside.

Divide filling into 20 equal parts, then place a part on each round. Fold dough over the filling and close by firmly pinching edges together into a half-moon or triangle shape. Place pies on well-greased baking trays, then bake in a 300° F (150° C) preheated oven for 1 hour or until pies turn golden brown. Remove from oven, brush with olive oil and serve.

Tepsi Badhinjan

—BISON AND VEGETABLE CASSEROLE

Serves about 6

This recipe is my version of one of the hundreds of dishes that are unique to Iraq. To explore further the richness of Iraqi cuisine and history, I recommend reading *Delights from the Garden of Eden: A Cookbook and a History of the Iraqi Cuisine*, by food historian Nawal Nasrallah. Containing more than four hundred recipes, each introduced by thoroughly researched historical and cultural narratives, it is the most comprehensive work in the English language to tell the fascinating story of the Iraqi kitchen.

1 lb / 454 g	eggplant
2 tsps / 10 ml	salt, divided
3	medium carrots (or 3 medium potatoes)
2	medium onions
3	medium tomatoes
½ cup / 125 ml	vegetable oil
1 lb / 454 g	ground bison
4	cloves garlic, crushed
1 tsp / 5 ml	pepper, divided
1 tsp / 5 ml	cumin, divided
⅛ tsp / ½ ml	cayenne
½ cup / 125 ml	water

Peel eggplant, then halve lengthwise and slice into half rounds about 1 inch (2.5 cm) thick. Place on a platter and sprinkle with ½ tsp (2 ml) of the salt and set aside.

Peel carrots. Cut carrots, onions and tomatoes into slices ½ inch (13 mm) thick. Set aside.

Heat oil in a frying pan, then fry eggplant slices over medium heat for about 8 minutes or until light golden, turning them over once and adding more oil if necessary. Drain on paper towels.

In the same oil, always adding more if necessary and stirring once in a while, lightly fry the carrots, then the onions, over medium heat for 10 minutes each. Set aside.

In the meantime, thoroughly combine ground bison, half the garlic, ½ tsp (2 ml) of the salt, ½ tsp (2 ml) of pepper, ½ tsp (2 ml) of the cumin, and cayenne, then form into small balls. Fry in the same frying pan over medium-low heat for 10 minutes, adding more oil if necessary and stirring once in a while. Set aside.

Combine water, the remaining salt, garlic, pepper and cumin, then set aside.

Arrange the eggplant pieces on the bottom of a casserole, then arrange evenly on top carrot rounds, onions and slices of tomatoes, in that order. Spread meatballs evenly between the tomato slices, then pour water mixture on top. Cover and bake in a 300° F (150° C) preheated oven for 1¼ hours or until balls are well cooked, then serve hot from the casserole.

saneeyat ruzz, laham wa laban
—RICE, BISON AND YOGURT CASSEROLE

Serves about 8

An ancient wonder food, yogurt is considered to be powerfully antibacterial. Modern nutritionists have established that its medicinal reputation is justified. Yogurt has been found to contain a digestive enzyme that prolongs life. Humans naturally produce this enzyme in their childhood, but become deficient in it as they reach adulthood.

In addition to the healthful elements found in milk, yogurt contains a teeming load of bacteria—about 100 million per gram. These multiply in the intestines and spur the activity of natural killer cells that attack viruses and tumours, help to get rid of accumulated germs, aid in relieving stomach ulcers and dysentery, fight bone problems such as osteoporosis and yeast infections in women and promote excellent digestion. Above all, yogurt helps to neutralize cancer-causing agents in the intestinal tract and is safe for people with lactose intolerance.

Much more easily digestible than milk, yogurt is ideal for the aged, pregnant women, children and the sick. In addition, it is believed that regular eaters of this fermented milk tend to have clear skin and find no problem in enjoying a good night's sleep. Also, in a recent study, Japanese researchers have found that eating traditional yogurt reduces the malodorous compounds that cause bad breath.

For maximum taste, this dish should be served hot from the casserole.

1 lb / 454 g	bison round steak
2 tsps / 10 ml	olive oil
2	medium onions, finely chopped
4	cloves garlic, crushed
1 cup / 250 ml	rice
6 cups / 1500 ml	water
2 cups / 500 ml	plain yogurt
1 tsp / 5 ml	dried crushed mint
1 tsp / 5 ml	salt
1 tsp / 5 ml	baking soda
½ tsp / 2 ml	pepper
1	egg, beaten

Cut bison steak into ½-inch (13-mm) cubes.

Heat oil in a frying pan, then sauté bison meat, onions and garlic over medium-low heat for 10 minutes. Set aside and allow to cool.

In the meantime, place rice and water in a pot, then bring to a boil. Cover and cook over medium heat for 8 minutes, then drain rice and allow to cool.

Place rice in a bowl, then stir in the contents of the frying pan and the remaining ingredients. Mix well, then transfer to a casserole. Bake in a 300° F (150° C) preheated oven for 1½ to 2 hours or until meat is tender.

molokhia —SPANISH OKRA

Serves 8 to 10

Molokhia—also *meloukhia, melokhiya* or *milookhiyya*—is a pot-herb that is better known in the English-speaking world as Spanish okra or Jew's mallow. Its reputed land of origin is India, but it has always been widely grown in the Middle East and parts of Africa, especially Egypt and the Greater Syria area. Said to have been the favourite food of the ancient Egyptians, it is an exceptionally healthy green-leaf green—called by some "the queen of vegetables."

In Egypt *molokhia* continues to be a preferred food of rich and poor alike. Almost every housewife of whatever strata in society prepares *molokhia* daily. The rich cook it with meat and the poor with other vegetables. *Molokhia* is so much in demand there that every farmer grows his little patch for his own use or for sale.

This recipe, usually made with chicken, is a favourite of many, and variations of it are cooked in all the Greater Syria area of the Middle East. It is just as delicious when made with bison meat.

If *molokhia* is not available, spinach makes an excellent replacement.

3 lbs / 1.36 kg	bison round steak, cut into serving pieces
10 cups / 2.5 L	water
1 tsp / 5 ml	cinnamon
4	bay leaves
1	medium onion, chopped into large pieces
½	head garlic, crushed
½ cup / 125 ml	butter
4 Tbsp / 60 ml	finely chopped coriander leaves
1 lb / 454 g	fresh *molokhia* leaves
2 tsps / 10 ml	salt
1 tsp / 5 ml	pepper
4 Tbsp / 60 ml	lemon juice
1	loaf Arab (pita) bread, toasted and broken into small pieces
	cooked rice

Place bison steak in a saucepan with the water, cinnamon, bay leaves and onion, then cook over medium-low heat for 1 hour or until meat is barely tender. Remove meat with a slotted spoon, then set aside.

Strain stock, then return it to the saucepan and set aside.

In a frying pan, sauté garlic in butter over medium-low heat for 1 minute, then add coriander leaves and bison meat and sauté over medium heat until meat is lightly browned. Remove meat and place on a platter, ready to serve.

Add *molokhia,* salt, pepper and lemon juice to stock, then bring to a boil. Cook uncovered on medium heat for 25 minutes, then cover the pot. Turn off the heat and let stand for 20 minutes, then transfer cooked *molokhia* to a serving bowl.

When serving, place a handful of toasted bread on each plate, then place a layer of rice on top of bread. Over this, place the *molokhia* with some of its juice, then one or more meat pieces.

NOTE: *For heightened taste, make a mixture consisting of ½ cup (125 ml) of table vinegar and one medium finely-chopped Spanish onion, then place one to two tablespoons of this mixture (to taste) over the* molokhia *for each serving.*

Ruzz Jaari —RICE AND BISON

Serves about 4

This dish originating in Libya is usually made with lamb, but tender bison meat makes a fine replacement.

For travellers, true Libyan food can usually be found only if one is invited to a Libyan home. In Libya's small towns, visitors will find very few restaurants, usually serving very simple food. In the larger cities the better restaurants have on their menu an international cuisine. The Libyans themselves prefer to eat at home. Eating at restaurants is uncommon, even for the residents of large cities.

If guests are present at a meal, they are always served first. The woman of the house places platters of food on the table and the guests are expected to eat by helping themselves from around the edges of the platters. The host and the family, as well as the guests, eat by using the fingers of the right hand to scoop up the food.

½ lb / 227 g	bison round steak
4 Tbsp / 60 ml	butter
1 cup / 250 ml	rice
1 Tbsp / 15 ml	tomato paste
2¼ cups / 560 ml	water
¼ tsp / 1 ml	cumin
¼ tsp / 1 ml	ground coriander seeds
½ tsp / 2 ml	salt

Cut bison steak into ½-inch (13-mm) cubes.

Melt butter in a frying pan, then sauté bison meat over medium-low heat for 15 minutes, stirring often. Add rice, then stir-fry for 1 minute. Dilute tomato paste in the water, then add to frying pan along with remaining ingredients. Bring to a boil, then cover and cook over medium-low heat for 20 minutes, stirring a number of times to make sure rice does not stick to bottom of pan. Turn off heat, then re-cover and allow to cook in its own steam for 30 minutes.

Laham Mufalful bi Habbat al-Barakah
—SPICY BISON

Serves 4

Black cumin (or, as it is sometimes called, black caraway) is still a relatively unknown herb/spice in the Western world. Known in the Arab lands as *Habbat al-Sawda* (the black seed) or *Habbat al-Barakah* (the seed of blessing) because of the many powerful healing qualities attributed to it, black cumin (*negilla sativa*) has been used for centuries by chefs and herbalists for enhancing food and for treating a whole series of ailments.

2 lbs / 907 g	bison round steak
6 Tbsp / 90 ml	butter
½ tsp / 2 ml	black cumin seeds
2	medium onions, finely chopped
4	cloves garlic, crushed
1 tsp / 5 ml	salt
½ tsp / 2 ml	ground coriander seeds
½ tsp / 2 ml	ground ginger
⅛ tsp / ½ ml	cloves
¼ tsp / 1 ml	black pepper
½ cup / 125 ml	grape juice
2 cups / 500 ml	water

Cut bison steak into ½-inch (13-mm) cubes.

Melt butter in a saucepan, then sauté bison meat over medium-low heat for 10 minutes, stirring a few times. Remove meat with slotted spoon and set aside.

Add black cumin seeds to butter, then stir-fry until seeds begin to crackle, about one minute. Add onions, then stir-fry over medium-low heat for 10 minutes. Stir in remaining ingredients, including the bison meat, then bring to a boil and cover. Simmer over medium-low heat for about 1 hour or until the meat is cooked, adding more water if necessary. Serve hot with cooked rice or mashed potatoes.

Tajine —SPINACH AND BEAN PIE

Serves about 8 as an entree

Unlike most Middle Eastern and North African cuisines, Tunisian food is noted for its spicy hotness. It is said that a husband will judge his wife by the number of hot peppers with which she prepares her food. Some even believe that if a wife's cooking becomes bland, it means that her love for her husband is fading. On the other hand, when food is prepared for visitors, the amount of hot pepper is decreased to suit the typically more delicate palates of guests. *Hareesa*, a hot spice sauce, is served with every meal in order that hot dishes can be made even hotter, according to each diner's taste.

Tajines in Tunisia differ from those in Morocco. In Morocco *tajines* are types of stews, while in Tunisia they are types of soft pies.

4 Tbsp / 60 ml	olive oil
½ lb / 227 g	bison round steak, cut into very small pieces
2	medium onions, finely chopped
4	cloves garlic, crushed
1	small hot pepper, finely chopped
4 Tbsp / 60 ml	tomato paste
19 oz / 540 ml	white kidney beans, canned, not drained
1½ tsps / 7 ml	salt
1 tsp / 5 ml	oregano
½ tsp / 2 ml	pepper
½ tsp / 2 ml	cumin
2 cups / 500 ml	water
4 Tbsp / 60 ml	butter
10 oz / 284 g	spinach, thoroughly washed and chopped
½ cup / 125 ml	grated white cheese, any type
6	eggs, beaten

Heat oil in a frying pan, then sauté bison steak over medium-low heat for 5 minutes. Add onions, garlic and hot pepper, then stir-fry for a further 10 minutes. Stir in tomato paste, beans, salt, oregano, pepper, cumin and water, then bring to a boil. Cover, then cook over low heat for 1 hour or until meat is well cooked, adding a little more water if necessary.

In the meantime, melt butter in another frying pan, then stir-fry spinach until it wilts. Stir in the contents of the two frying pans, together with the cheese and eggs, into a casserole, then place in a 300° F (150° C) preheated oven. Cover and bake for 45 minutes, then uncover and bake for a further 15 minutes.

NOTE: *Excellent for appetizers or snacks, as a side dish or as an entree.*

κubba† Ruzz —RICE OVAL PATTIES

Makes about 20 kubbas

The foods of Iraq reflect the country's rich culinary inheritance as well as strong influences from the culinary traditions of Turkey and Iran and the Greater Syria area. Iraqi cuisine is thus enormously rich and varied. This *kubba,* a favourite in Iraq but a little spicier, is one of the few *kubbas* found in the Middle Eastern countries that does not use *burghul* as a main ingredient.

STUFFING

3 Tbsp / 45 ml	butter
½ lb / 227 g	ground bison
3 Tbsp / 45 ml	pine nuts or chopped walnuts
1	medium onion, finely chopped
½ tsp / 2 ml	salt
¼ tsp / 1 ml	black pepper
¼ tsp / 1 ml	allspice
¼ tsp / 1 ml	nutmeg

KUBBAT RUZZ DOUGH

3 cups / 750 ml	cooked rice
1½ lb / 680 g	ground bison
2 tsps / 10 ml	salt
1 tsp / 5 ml	black pepper
½ tsp / 2 ml	allspice
½ cup / 125 ml	flour
2 Tbsp / 30 ml	olive oil
1 tsp / 5 ml	cumin
¼ tsp / 1 ml	cayenne
	cooking oil

To prepare the stuffing, in a frying pan melt butter, then sauté ground bison over medium-low heat for 5 minutes. Stir in pine nuts or walnuts, onion, salt, pepper, allspice and nutmeg, then sauté further until onion is limp. Set aside.

To prepare the *kubbat ruzz* dough, place rice in food processor, then process until dough-like. Add ground bison, salt, pepper, allspice, flour, olive oil, cumin and cayenne, then process until a smooth but firm dough is formed, adding a little flour or water if necessary.

For each *kubba,* take enough *kubbat ruzz* dough to form a ball the size of a golf ball. Hold the ball in the palm of one hand. Using a forefinger, press a hole and begin expanding the hole by rotating and pressing against the palm until you have a shell of ¼-inch (6-mm) thickness. Place a heaping tablespoon of stuffing into the hollow shell. Close end of shell, then form into an egg shape. (Use cold water on hands to help shape and close shells.)

In saucepan, pour cooking oil to about 2 inches (5 cm) deep. Bring to medium heat, then deep-fry *kubba,* turning until golden brown. Serve hot.

OUZI —SQUARE MEAT PIES (DAMASCUS VERSION)

Makes 12 pies

This recipe follows the method for making *ouzi* in Damascus, the oldest continuously inhabited city on earth today. The Byzantine Emperor Justinian called Damascus "the light of the Orient." The writer Maurice Barrès is reported to have said, "Damascus is not a mere area of land; it is the place of the soul." It is said that the Prophet Muhammad refused to enter Damascus, which he considered "heaven on earth." He preferred to enter Paradise only once. Such is the history and reputation of this great city; through the centuries, Aramaeans, Assyrians, Persians, Greeks, Romans, Byzantines and, above all, the Umayyad Arabs of the seventh century, left a rich legacy in all areas of the city's daily life—including in its food.

In this "Damascus version" of *ouzi*, I have utilized many more spices than are usually used. If one finds it too spicy, some of these can be omitted.

24	sheets filo dough
4 Tbsp / 60 ml	olive oil
1 cup / 250 ml	ground bison
1	medium onion, finely chopped
4	cloves garlic, crushed
4 Tbsp / 60 ml	finely chopped coriander leaves
1 tsp / 5 ml	salt
½ tsp / 2 ml	pepper
½ tsp / 2 ml	cumin
½ tsp / 2 ml	allspice
¼ tsp / 1 ml	cinnamon
⅛ tsp / ½ ml	cayenne
1 cup / 250 ml	frozen or fresh peas
2 cups / 500 ml	cooked rice
½ cup / 125 ml	pine nuts or slivered almonds, toasted
½ cup / 125 ml	melted butter

Cut sheets of filo dough in half, then cover them with a slightly damp cloth.

Heat olive oil in a large frying pan, then sauté ground bison and onion over medium-low heat for 12 minutes. Add garlic, coriander leaves, salt, pepper, cumin, allspice, cinnamon and cayenne, then sauté for a further 3 minutes. Transfer to a mixing bowl, then stir in peas, rice and nuts to make a filling. Divide into 12 portions and set aside.

Brush 4 half-sheets of filo dough lightly with butter, then stack. Place one portion of filling in the middle then fold the filo dough over the filling from all sides to make a square pie. Continue until the 12 pies are done. Place in a greased baking pan, then brush with remaining butter. Bake in a 300° F (150° C) preheated oven for 1 hour or until the pies begin to brown. Serve warm.

spinach with ground bison

Serves about 6

It is believed that spinach is native to Persia, spreading from there to both the East and the West. It has been utilized as a food in China from at least the 7th century BCE, where it has been known as "the Persian herb." However, for reasons unknown, it was never cultivated in the Greek and Roman worlds. Europe had to wait until the eleventh century CE to become familiar with this green. Introduced into the Iberian peninsula by the Arabs, who were enamoured with its taste and healthful qualities, spinach was called the "prince of vegetables" and was rhapsodized in verse and stories. From Spain its cultivation spread to the remainder of Europe. Almost all the European languages derive their names for spinach from the Spanish *espinaca*, which in turn originated from the Arabic *isbanakh*. During the Middle Ages it was known as "the Spanish vegetable" and became much sought after as a Lenten food.

6 Tbsp / 90 ml	cooking oil
1 lb / 454 g	ground bison
1	large onion, finely chopped
4	cloves garlic, crushed
½ cup / 125 ml	finely chopped coriander leaves
2 cups / 500 ml	stewed tomatoes
1½ tsps / 7 ml	salt
1 tsp / 5 ml	pepper
1 tsp / 5 ml	ground cumin
⅛ tsp / ½ ml	cayenne
2½ cups / 625 ml	water
1 lb / 454 g	spinach, thoroughly washed and chopped
2 Tbsp / 30 ml	lemon juice

Heat oil in a saucepan, then fry ground bison over medium-low heat for 5 minutes, stirring occasionally. Stir in onion, garlic and coriander leaves, then fry over medium-low heat for a further 10 minutes, stirring often. Stir in tomatoes, salt, pepper, cumin, cayenne and water. Cover, then cook over medium-low heat for 1 hour, stirring occasionally and adding a little water if necessary. Add spinach, then cook over medium-low heat for a further 10 minutes, stirring often and adding a little water if necessary. Stir in lemon juice and serve hot.

Maqlooba —UPSIDE-DOWN EGGPLANT AND BISON DISH

Serves about 6

Eggplant cultivation spread only gradually into Western lands. In many parts of Europe it was near the end of the sixteenth century before it was widely grown and, then, mostly as a decorative plant. In North America, only in the last few decades has it been cultivated in an appreciable quantity, mainly in the southern United States. Requiring long warm summers to mature, eggplants thrive best in the tropical parts of the world. They grow from one to two feet high and produce wide grey-green leaves and fruits weighing from a few ounces to over two pounds. In the West, eggplants are cultivated for both culinary and ornamental purposes. However, in the East they are raised mostly for their edible fruit.

1 lb / 454 g	eggplant
1½ tsps / 7 ml	salt, divided
1 lb / 454 g	bison sirloin steak
½ cup / 125 ml	olive oil
4 Tbsp / 60 ml	butter
2	medium onions, finely chopped
¼ cup / 60 ml	pine nuts
4	cloves garlic, crushed
3 cups / 750 ml	boiling water, divided
1 cup / 250 ml	rice, rinsed
1 tsp / 5 ml	cumin
½ tsp / 2 ml	pepper
½ tsp / 2 ml	allspice

Without peeling, slice eggplant into slices ½ inch (13 mm) thick. Place slices in a strainer, then sprinkle with 1 tsp (5 ml) of the salt. Top with a weight, then allow to drain for 45 minutes.

Cut bison steak into ½-inch (13-mm) cubes.

Heat oil in a frying pan, then sauté eggplant slices over medium-high heat until they begin to brown, adding more oil if necessary. Remove, then drain on paper towels.

Melt the butter in a saucepan, then sauté meat, onions, pine nuts and garlic over medium-low heat for 10 minutes, stirring often. Add 1½ cups (375 ml) of the boiling water, then simmer on low heat until the water is almost absorbed. Place eggplant slices over meat, then spread rice evenly overtop.

Mix remaining 1½ cups (375 ml) of water with the remaining ½ tsp (2 ml) of salt, cumin, pepper and allspice, then pour over the rice. Cover, then cook over low heat for 20 minutes. Turn off heat, then allow to cook in its own steam for 30 minutes.

Just before serving, invert the serving platter over top of the saucepan, then hold securely and turn saucepan over, so that the rice is at the bottom and the meat on the top of the platter. Serve immediately.

mahshi falafli —STUFFED PEPPERS

Serves 6

Known to the Greeks as *dolmath,* to the Turks as *dolma,* to the Persians as *dolmeh,* and to the Arabs as *mahshi,* stuffed vegetables have been a favoured food in the Middle East and in the Balkans for centuries. It is believed that their origins go back to the ancient Middle East and Greece, where stuffed leaves of fig, hazelnut or mulberry trees and a number of vegetables became part of the daily meal.

However, the Turkish upper classes were the ones who refined these dishes and developed them into the cuisine of sultans. The elaborate preparation required to ready them for the pot made stuffed vegetables the specialty of the affluent. They became known as "the food of aristocrats" and were, for centuries, the top culinary delights in the grand banquets of the Turkish court.

For this recipe, a mixture of red and green peppers makes for a colourful dish.

6	large sweet peppers	Cut out stem ends of peppers and reserve. Remove seeds and fibres from peppers and discard. Set peppers aside.
2 tsps / 10 ml	garlic powder	
½ tsp / 2 ml	salt	
2 cups / 500 ml	tomato juice	Stir in garlic powder and salt to tomato juice and set aside.
1 lb / 454 g	ground bison	
½ cup / 125 ml	rice	Combine remaining ingredients to make stuffing.
2	medium tomatoes, finely chopped	
1	medium onion, finely chopped	Stuff peppers, then close with stem ends. Arrange to fit tightly in a saucepan with the openings on top. Add tomato juice mixture to the saucepan, along with enough water to reach the top of the peppers. Bring to a boil, then cover and cook over medium-low heat for 1¼ hours or until peppers are done. Serve hot with sauce.
4 Tbsp / 60 ml	finely chopped coriander leaves	
4 Tbsp / 60 ml	olive oil	
1½ tsps / 7 ml	salt	
½ tsp / 2 ml	pepper	
½ tsp / 2 ml	cumin	
½ tsp / 2 ml	allspice	
⅛ tsp / ½ ml	cayenne	

Brik —TUNISIAN MEAT AND EGG PIE

Makes 8 pies

The Tunisian cuisine is a true mixture of East and West. It has borrowed much from the neighbouring Mediterranean countries and the previous civilizations that once thrived in that land. Phoenicians, Romans, Arabs, Andalusian-Arabs, Turks, French and the native Berbers all contributed to the creation of the modern Tunisian kitchen, unique among the cuisines of the world.

Briks, of Turkish origin, are as popular in Tunisia as hamburgers are in North America. They are sold in small restaurants or from *brik* stands and are prepared almost routinely by Tunisian housewives.

9	small eggs
4 Tbsp / 60 ml	butter
½ lb / 227 g	ground bison
1	medium onion, finely chopped
2	cloves garlic, crushed
4 Tbsp / 60 ml	finely chopped coriander leaves
1	small hot pepper, finely chopped
1 tsp / 5 ml	salt
1 tsp / 5 ml	cumin
½ tsp / 2 ml	pepper
4 Tbsp / 60 ml	crumbled feta cheese
8	sheets of filo dough
	oil for frying

Beat one of the eggs in a small bowl, then set aside.

To make filling, melt butter in a frying pan, then sauté ground bison over medium-low heat for 10 minutes. Stir in onion, garlic, coriander leaves, hot pepper, salt, cumin and pepper, then stir-fry for a further 8 minutes. Remove from heat, then stir in cheese and set aside to cool.

Take a sheet of filo dough and fold twice to make a square, then place ⅛ of the filling on the centre and make a well in the filling. Brush edges of square with some of the beaten egg, then break an egg into the well. Fold one corner over diagonally to meet the opposite corner and form a triangle, then press the edges together to seal, in the process turning the edges a little to make certain the *briks* are well-sealed.

Place oil in a frying pan to a depth of about 1 inch (2.5 cm), then heat. Gently slide the *brik* into the heated oil and fry over medium-low heat, turning over once so that both sides turn golden brown. Continue the same process until all the *briks* are done. Serve immediately. If not served immediately, the *briks* will become soggy and lose much of their appeal.

tajine bil laham jamus —HOT BISON CASSEROLE

Serves 6

In Libya, as in the other North African countries, *tajine* is a basic dish. The meats used are lamb, chicken or beef. Pork is not consumed by the inhabitants of North Africa, since these are Muslim countries. All other meat must be *halal* (meaning that the meat has been slaughtered in the manner prescribed by Muslim law). Alongside meat, other staples of the Libyan diet are olive oil, beans, rice, nuts, pasta, semolina, dates, dried apricots, figs and unleavened bread.

4 Tbsp / 60 ml	butter, melted
2 lbs / 907 g	bison sirloin steak, cut into large serving pieces
3 Tbsp / 45 ml	tomato paste
2 cups / 500 ml	hot water
3	medium carrots, sliced into thin rounds
1½ tsps / 7 ml	salt
1 tsp / 5 ml	garlic powder
1 tsp / 5 ml	black pepper
½ tsp / 2 ml	cumin
½ tsp / 2 ml	ground ginger
½ tsp / 2 ml	ground coriander seeds
¼ tsp / 1 ml	chilli pepper
10	pitted black olives

Melt butter in a frying pan, then sauté bison steak over medium-low heat for 10 minutes. Transfer to a casserole and set aside.

Dilute tomato paste in the 2 cups (500 ml) of hot water, then add remaining ingredients, except olives. Pour over meat. Cover, then place in a 300° F (150° C) preheated oven and bake for 2 hours. Spread olives over top and re-cover, then bake for a further 15 minutes. Serve hot with cooked rice or couscous.

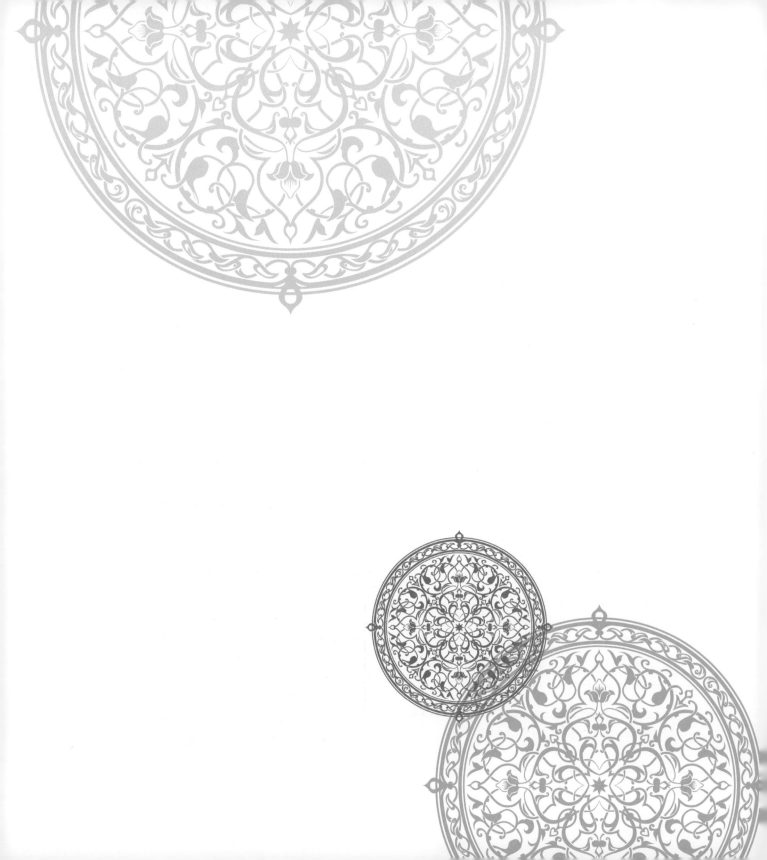

selected reading list

BOOKS

Danz, Harold P. *Of Bison and Man: From the Annals of a Bison Yesterday to a Refreshing Outcome from Human Involvement with America's Most Valiant of Beasts.* Niwot, CO: University Press of Colorado, 1997.

Foster, John, Dick Harrison, and I.S. McLaren, eds. *Buffalo.* Alberta Nature and Culture Series. Edmonton, AB: University of Alberta Press, 1992.

Franke, Mary Ann. *To Save the Wild Bison: Life on the Edge in Yellowstone.* Norman, OK: University of Oklahoma Press, 2005.

Geist, Valerius. *Buffalo Nation: History and Legend of the North American Bison.* Stillwater, MN: Voyageur Press Inc., 1996.

Indian and Northern Affairs Canada. *Remarkable Recipes for Sweet-Grass Buffalo: Canada's Northwest Territories / Recettes pour le gourmet bison du nord-ouest canadien.* Ottawa, Queen's Printer: 1961.

Isenberg, Andrew C. *The Destruction of the Bison: An Environmental History, 1750–1920.* Cambridge: Cambridge University Press, 2000.

Johnston, Ruth M. *The Buffalo Cookbook: The Low Fat Solution to Eating Red Meat.* Surrey, BC: Hancock House Publishers Ltd., 1995.

Lott, Dale F. *American Bison: A Natural History.* Los Angeles: University of California Press Ltd., 2002.

Mallos, Tess. *The Complete Middle East Cookbook.* North Clarendon, VT: Tuttle Publishing, 2006.

Mardam-Bey, Farouk. *Ziryab: Authentic Arab Cuisine.* Woodbury, CT: Ici La Press, 2002.

Nasrallah, Nawal. *Delights from the Garden of Eden: A Cookbook and a History of the Iraqi Cuisine.* Authorhouse, 2003.

Nelson, Kay Shaw. *The Yogurt Cookbook.* Mineola, NY: Dover Publications, 1977.

Olson, Wes. *Portraits of the Bison: An Illustrated Guide to Bison Society.* Edmonton, AB: University of Alberta Press, 2005.

Picton, Harold. *Buffalo: Natural History and Conservation.* Stillwater, MN: Voyageur Press, 2005.

Punke, Michael. *Last Stand: George Bird Grinnell, the Battle to Save the Buffalo, and the Birth of the New West.* New York: Smithsonian Books/Collins, 2007.

Rudner, Ruth. *A Chorus of Buffalo: A Personal Portrait of an American Icon.* New York: Marlowe and Co., 2000.

Shaykh ᶜUmar Abu Muhammad. *The Perfumed Garden of the Shaykh Nefzawi.* New York: Castle Books, 1964.

Wright, Clifford A. *A Mediterranean Feast: The Story of the Birth of the Celebrated Cuisines of the Mediterranean from the Merchants of Venice to the Barbary Corsairs, with More than 500 Recipes.* William Morrow and Company, Inc: New York, 1999.

Zontek, Ken. *Buffalo Nation: American Indian Efforts to Restore the Bison.* Lincoln: University of Nebraska Press, 2007.

SITES ON THE WEB:

www.canadianbison.ca/producer/The_CBA/the_association.htm

www.canadianbison.ca/consumer/default.aspx

www.pbs.org/wnet/nature/buffalo

www.bisoncentral.com

www.centurygamepark.com/romance.htm

home.centurytel.net/DoubleRBison/poetry.htm

www.merceronline.com/Native/native05.htm

www.ebabison.org

www.wibison.com/about_bison.iml

www.firstpeople.us/FP-Html-Wisdom/ChiefPlentyCoups.html

www.northforkbison.com

index